"What might your name be?"

"Hardy."

"Of Brewer?"

"It is."

In the 1800s the Hardy name was well known across Maine and beyond. Manly Hardy was a fur trapper, trader, friend of the Indians, ornithologist, and an expert woodsman.

His daughter, Fannie, would become one of Maine's most famous early period historians on the ways of the woods, the outdoors, and co-editor of texts documenting folk songs and ballads.

Father and daughter left a legacy of Maine stories in their writing that serve to educate and remind us of what it was like before Maine was populated, when there were still log drives, and lumbermen came to town. It was a time before maps could be counted on; a time when the knowledge of woodcraft was king when it came to the Maine woods.

This book is a story of a father-daughter canoe trip to the Machias Lakes Region. It is a memoir of exploring, observing, and interpreting for those who would follow; and more importantly, for those who would never see these lakes, ponds, and carries, as they were, then, in the fall of 1890.

A

Burnt Jacket Publishing

Classic Release

Exploring
The Maine Woods

——

The Hardy Family Expedition
to the
Machias Lakes

Fannie Pearson Hardy Eckstorm

based on the 1891 articles published in
FOREST AND STREAM
"IN THE REGION ROUND NICATOWIS"

Annotated Edition
by Tommy Carbone, Ph.D.

ANNOTATED EDITION

Cover photo, and newly added interior illustrations, and photos from the collection of Tommy Carbone, or as otherwise noted.

Eckstorm back cover portrait (June 1888) courtesy Special Collections, Raymond H. Fogler Library, Univ. of Maine.

Cover and book design by Tommy Carbone.

Author of new material and edition editor, Tommy Carbone.

Burnt Jacket Publishing
Greenville, Maine

ISBN: 978-1-954048-07-2

20210529 ISHCDJ
Also available in
Case Laminate Hardcover
Paperback

www.tommycarbone.com

1. Maine woods - 2. Canoeing - 3. Camping –
4. Expeditions and adventure - 5. Memoir - 6. Naturalist –
7. Hunting and fishing. - 8. Woodsmen –
9. 19th Century History - 10. Downeast Maine.

Contents

ANNOTATED EDITION PHOTOGRAPHS

About the advertisements

In the days books such as this were originally published, they included many advertisements as sponsorship to the cost of printing. In this book, advertisements have been selected from the time period that would have been found in magazines such as *Forest and Stream*. While the establishments no longer exist, they provide a stamp on the period of Maine history and add to the nostalgia of the writing.

INTRODUCTION

Memoirs and books on exploring Maine have been popular with readers and visitors for centuries. *The Maine Woods (1864),* by Henry Thoreau, might have been the book that put the north woods of Maine on the literary map, and others were soon to follow. Some of the earliest of these were guidebooks of the 1800s, written by Way, Hubbard, Farrar, and Steele. Into the first half of the twentieth century, Donn Fendler's 1939 account of his days lost near Katahdin gripped the nation; Helen Hamlin told of her early years at a remote camp in the 1930s; and in 1942, Louise Dickinson Rich told us of her life-lived in the woods.

A writer less known for her memoir of exploring the Maine woods is Fannie Hardy Eckstorm. This is not because Mrs. Eckstorm wasn't well known in Maine and beyond, she certainly was a force in Maine history, as the reader will discover. However, her memoir essay of her trip to the Maine woods has not been widely available. She did not publish a book based on her writing, and so her wonderful story has not been easy to locate. The purpose of this book is to introduce more readers to Eckstorm, so they may discover her writing and the Maine woods she loved.

In the 1800s, the magazine *Forest and Stream* included a weekly section titled, "The Sportsman Tourist," which ran contributed articles for the hunter, fisherman, and explorer. In 1891, Fannie Pearson Hardy[1] submitted a series titled, "In The Region Round Nicatowis." The essays form a memoir of a father-daughter three-week long canoe trip in the Maine woods. This book is based on that series of articles.

---

[1] The articles were published two years prior to her marriage under her maiden name, Fannie Pearson Hardy.

The area of Maine where this story takes place extends from Enfield in the west to Third Machias Lake in the east. The Hardy paddling itinerary began at Nicatous Stream, down to Nicatous Lake, over to Gassabias Lake and then they carried to the Machias chain of lakes. They then returned to Pistol Green and continued on the Passadumkeag River northwards, from which they made their way to Upper Sysladobsis Lake.[2]

The purpose of their trip, I suspect, was not solely for a three week 'camping adventure.' And while, Manly Hardy was an expert fur trader, ornithologist, and an explorer of the woods, this trip was not a trapping or hunting excursion. At the time of year they traveled, late September into October, the forest bird population would have declined and by this time in his life, Mr. Hardy had already accumulated a good portion of the 3,300 bird species in his collection. Rather, from analyzing Manly Hardy's journals it is discovered that beginning in the year Fannie Hardy graduated from college, a multi-week canoe trip became an annual tradition with the father and daughter. In August and September of 1888, they traveled the East Branch of the Penobscot. The following August of 1889 they canoed the West Branch. September and October of 1890 found them on the Passadumkeag River to the Machias Lakes. And then in the spring of 1891, they made the trip across Moosehead and down the West Branch to Ripogenus.

It is very likely that Mr. Hardy was further exposing his daughter to the "ways of the woods," a subject she would feel strongly about for the rest of her life. The experiences also enabled Mrs. Eckstorm to gather material and photographs for what would become her book, "The Penobscot Man."

---

[2] In this introduction, I have used the current names of locations.

Their longer trips, and the many other short excursions to the deep north woods, the Downeast forests, and the Maine coast were opportunities for Fannie Hardy to learn from her father. The two developed a supportive relationship of intellectual and outdoor interests that through their combined writings provided us a wealth of knowledge about Maine woods history.

The fall the Hardy's paddled the Passadumkeag River, down through Nicatous, and the chain of the Machias Lakes, the area was much less populated than today. Even though much of this land is now protected forest, and undeveloped, the maps of 1890 were incomplete, and as Manly Hardy might have said, "the maps are wrong." They traveled at a time when exploring in these remote woods was considered an expedition, full of unknowns. In the first chapter, Eckstorm hints, likely knowing what was to come from their prior trips, "no premonition warned us how we should yet be fed."

They were traveling away from civilization in the cities of Brewer and Bangor, and to eat, meant they had to hunt and fish. If they were not successful, they'd go hungry.

For the most part, they lived off the land; even if that meant pickerel for breakfast, lunch, and dinner. They slept on beds made from fresh cut evergreen boughs. The weather was as uncooperative as the game, and many days and nights were soggy. Even so, there were no complaints, the Maine woods was where they wanted to be, where they enjoyed being, no matter the inconveniences.

The Nicatous Lake region, even then, was not as remote as the north woods of Maine (meaning north of the Golden Road and beyond Katahdin), but in 1890 once reaching the fork of the Passadumkeag and the Nicatous Stream, and certainly by Fourth Lake, it would have seemed as remote as the Allagash.

The writing is descriptive, the connections Mrs. Eckstorm makes are enlightening, the stories of the people they met and the included remembrances of other Mainers make this book much more than an essay of a canoe sightseeing trip. The story is about the ways of life and traditions in this region of the Maine woods at the time; a time the Hardys knew would be changing, if not already, from what they had known. They went to explore, they went to remember, and this book now allows us to relive their travels of so long ago.

Releasing a book, such as this one, with many historical names of places and people, along with the stories some of the woodsmen told, is sure to elicit emotion from 'scholars' who claim the naming of places, or the attributions from Mrs. Eckstorm are incorrect, incomplete or unsubstantiated. I do not care to argue about these items. Mrs. Eckstorm and her father were well respected in their knowledge of the woods during their time, so who are we to question that expertise?

As to her father, Manly, the editors of *Forest and Stream* always respected his opinion, and in 1901 wrote this about him, "No one is more familiar with the wild animals of Maine than Mr. Manly Hardy, the veteran woodsman and traveler of Brewer, Me."[3] In the biographical sketch of Manly Hardy you will see he was known as someone who didn't let an error pass without correction to set the record straight.

Like father, like daughter, Eckstorm was apt to do the same when the situation called for it. Her letter about the name of Lobster Lake, which I have included in the Appendix, is one such example.

Eckstorm's writing stands as a testament to what was, what the Hardy family knew at the time, and what they were kind enough to write down for us to enjoy. When I discovered the articles Mrs. Eckstorm had written, I was surprised she had never published a book about this trip. The themes and the quality of her storytelling rival the Maine woods memoirs of the age by Hubbard or Steele. I suspect a book on the trip

---

[3] Hardy, M, "No Panthers in Maine." Forest and Stream, Vol. 56, pg. 25 (1901). Magazine editor comments prior to Hardy's response to a query on Panthers in Maine.

wasn't her objective, and she moved on from this project, so as to focus on her main interests of ornithology and Maine Indian history. We can be certain that the Maine woods were her laboratory, where she accomplished so much research and amassed her experiences for her writing projects that were on the horizon in the years after this trip.

As to editing, in most of this book Eckstorm's original writing is left untouched, but corrections were made where required for the reader experience. Spellings of the 1890s remain as penned by in the original essays. In a handful of cases, I have corrected obvious printing errors. There were a couple of errata that were issued in following installments of the *Forest and Stream* articles, and those corrections have been made in this text.

Mrs. Eckstorm had a tendency to use many semicolons in her writing. This was indicative of the period; prior to this, a long dash was popular – often used to inject a parallel – and used in many books in the 1800s.

By 1930, the year E.B. White bought his small farm in Brooklin, due south of the Hardy homestead in Brewer, he had received the benefit of Professor William Strunk and *the little book*. But Mr. White wouldn't republish, *The Elements of Style*, until 1959. In this regard, please forgive Mrs. Eckstorm her excess " ; " while at the same time, please note in many cases I have edited the original work in the spirit of Strunk & White when it comes to the modern use of punctuation where appropriate, called for, and the writing seems to so dictate.

New to this edition are the inset annotations and all but one of the footnotes. In addition, chapter quotes and photographs are included that were not part of the original writing.

I am once again grateful to the wonderful staff of the Special Collections Department at the Fogler Library at the University of Maine in Orono. I especially want to thank, Ms. Desiree Butterfield-Nagy for her knowledge of the archives. From the Colby College Special Collections & Archives, I acknowledge the assistance of Ms. Patricia

Burdick. To my daughter, Gina, I thank her for her attention to detail on assisting with the editing for this book.

I am confident, you will enjoy the story Mrs. Eckstorm set out to tell, as much as I have. Publishing her story once again for others to discover has given me a great deal of satisfaction. It is doubly so, since during the research for this book I was alerted to the correspondence between Lucius L. Hubbard and Fannie Eckstorm. To find out she and her father knew Hubbard directly is a wonderful surprise. I will treasure having their books side by side, displayed on my Maine bookshelf. Enjoy the expedition.

Tommy Carbone, Ph.D.
Edition Editor
Greenville, Maine
April 2021

www.tommycarbone.com

FANNIE PEARSON HARDY ECKSTORM

(1865 – 1946)

The photo on the right was taken in 1888, the year of Eckstorm's college graduation, and two years prior to her writing the series of essays that are presented in this book.

Images courtesy of Special Collections, Raymond H. Fogler Library, University of Maine

Fannie Pearson Hardy Eckstorm was born on June 18, 1865, in Brewer, Maine to Manly Hardy and Emmeline Wheeler Hardy. She was the oldest of their six children and attended the public schools in Brewer, Maine and Abbot Academy (Andover, Massachusetts). In 1888, she graduated from Smith College (Northampton, Massachusetts), was subsequently employed as the superintendent of schools in Brewer, and for a time worked in the book department of the D.C. Heath Publishing Company in Boston.

In 1893 she married Rev. Jacob A. Eckstorm of Chicago. Seven years later, following the passing of her husband, Fannie Eckstorm and her two children relocated from Providence R.I., back to Brewer, Maine.

Throughout her life, Eckstorm studied Maine Indians, folklore and natural history. It was an area she knew well, based on her experiences with her father in the woods and her personal acquaintance with Indians and woodsmen. This book is only one example of her deep knowledge in these subjects.

In 1886 she became an associate member of the American Ornithologists Union, the first woman admitted as such. Before graduating Smith College, she co-founded the college chapter of the Audubon Society. Her interest in birds would be a lifelong pursuit, from which she published two books, *The Woodpeckers* (1901) and *The Bird Book* (1901).

She had a deep interest in documenting Maine folksongs and woods songs, and in collaboration with others, two books resulted from her efforts, *Minstrelsy of Maine* (1927) and *British Ballads from Maine* (1929).

Mrs. Eckstorm had many other community interests, among them, she was a founder and vice-president of the Folk-Song Society of the Northeast, a founding member of the public library in Brewer, and was an honorary member of the Maine Historical Society.

Over the years, while she did not compile the writings of her trip to Nicatowis as a book, she did publish the following:

- The Penobscot Man (1904).
- David Libbey: Penobscot Woodsman and River-Driver, (1907).
- Of Indian Place-Names of the Penobscot Valley and the Maine Coast (1941).
- Old John Neptune and Other Maine Indian Shamans (1945).

Mrs. Eckstorm also wrote for magazines such as *Forest and Stream*, *Sprague's Journal of Maine History*, *The Northern*, *The New England Quarterly*, *The Atlantic Monthly* and other publications and newspapers.

The essays that form the basis for this book were published in 1891, three years following Eckstorm's graduation from college. She was twenty six years old at the time.

The Special Collections Department at the Raymond H. Fogler Library of the University of Maine holds the, "Fannie Hardy Eckstorm Paper Collection, 1865-1946." Much of this material is available online. I am grateful, once again, for the help and assistance of the library staff with this project.

On December 31, 1946 Fannie Hardy Eckstorm passed away. She had been residing in the same home in Brewer since moving there in 1900. She was 81 years young.

I would have been honored to have known Fannie Hardy Eckstorm. I can only imagine what a night around the campfire would have been with her stories and Maine knowledge. I hope this book helps others discover the wonderful life and contributions of Mrs. Eckstorm.

MANLY HARDY

(1832 – 1910)

Manly Hardy was born on November 11, 1832, in Hampden, Maine, the only child of Jonathan Titcomb Hardy and Catherine Sears Atwood Hardy. The family moved to Brewer, Maine, when Manly was four, and he remained there for the rest of his life.

He attended the public schools, and for advanced studies attended the private school conducted by the Rev. George W. Field, D. D., in Bangor. Early in life Mr. Hardy injured his eyes (said to be from study at night), and for many years could not read at all. He was said to have a remarkable memory.

He became a fur buyer and dealer, maintaining one of the most extensive fur businesses in Maine. He spent much of his time in the woods of Maine, acquiring an expansive knowledge of woodlore and developing friendships with other men familiar with the wilderness, including the local Indians, to whom he could converse in their language. Overall, he was an expert woodsman.

He was a hunter of deer, moose and bear, and was also fond of hunting seals and porpoises from a canoe, a sport which was often dangerous, and likely always to be full of excitement. He made a long study of the ruffed grouse, and was one of the first authorities in the United States on this bird.

In 1861 he was the assistant naturalist on the Maine State Scientific Survey. He began to mount birds and assembled a collection of some 3,300 U.S. birds. He became the most widely known naturalist of Maine in his time, and was an honorary member of the Maine Ornithological Society. He also wrote extensively about the Maine woods, Indians, and mammals.

He married Emmeline Freeman Wheeler on December 24, 1862. They had six children: Fannie Hardy Eckstorm, Catherine Atwood Hardy Bates, Annie Eliza Hardy Eckstorm, Manly Willis Hardy, who lived less than two years, and twins Charlotte W. Hardy and Walter M. Hardy.

The following was written about him in a 1910 issue of *Forest and Stream*. "Mr. Hardy's stern love of truth has sometimes led him to correct sharply in print statements which he knew were incorrect, and it has been in such critical writings that his name has most often been seen. Yet it is not his nature to find fault. On the contrary, he is a genial, humorous and wholly friendly man, who would much rather praise than blame, yet, as we conceive, possesses the simple feeling that, no one is entitled to especial credit for telling the simple truth."

This quote is important because his daughter also called upon facts to correct what she saw as errors that writers had made. A few examples are given in this book.

While Manly Hardy kept meticulous journals and wrote several magazine pieces, Fannie Hardy Eckstorm wrote this about her father:

"Of his writing I may mention one characteristic. He never overstated. His two longest writings, each of which filled several installments of Forest and Stream, 'A Maine Woods Walk in '61' and 'A

Fall Fur Hunt,' might have been much expanded if he had chosen to dilate upon his incidents. But he condensed as much as possible even while telling a story. I remonstrated with him upon this. 'I didn't want to make the broth too thick,' was his characteristic response."

Manly Hardy died on December 9, 1910.

- - - - - - -

The information for the profile of Manly Hardy is from several sources, with the majority from a profile written by Mrs. Eckstorm in tribute to her father. Eckstorm, Fannie Hardy, "Manly Hardy," The Journal of the Maine Ornithological Society, Vol. XIII, No. I., March 1911, Pg. 1-9.

WALTER HARDY

Walter M. Hardy (1877 – 1933) was an artist, writer, and owner of a Maine apple orchard. The son of Manly Hardy, he was born in Brewer on February 9, 1877, and after graduating from Bangor High School in 1896, he spent a year at the University of Maine before transferring to the Art Students League in New York City. He also studied in Paris, England, and Italy. Like his father, he was interested in birds and other wildlife. After his return to the U.S., he did illustrations of birds and animals for various publications. He also illustrated some of the articles written by his father. In 1911, he bought a farm in Holden, Maine, where he planted a large apple orchard. He raised and sold apples there until his death on September 17, 1933.

ANNA BOYNTON AVERILL

In some of the chapters, quotes from the poems of Anna Boynton Averill (1843 – 1915) have been added. There is no connection (that the editor is aware of) between Ms. Averill and Mrs. Eckstorm other than the overlap in lifespans. I discovered the poetry of Ms. Averill in the edition of Forest and Stream of which Mrs. Eckstorm's essays first appeared. Averill's poems about the Maine north woods seemed appropriate for this book.

Averill, was an accomplished poet who had a large collection of her poems published in a book, "Birch Stream And Other Poems," (1908). She was born in Alton, Maine and as of the 1870 census was employed as a teacher and living in the town of Dover in Piscataquis County.

THE NICATOWIS LAKE REGION OF MAINE

Area Of 1890 Expedition – Nicatowis Lake

MAP AREA OF THE EXPEDITION

No one map from the time period of 1890 could be located for the region the Hardy's explored. This map image is a composite of the Hubbard Map, a mid-1800s map of Hancock County, and drawn additions. There are obvious flaws, besides the composite rendition and the differing scales.

For example, Saponac Lake is not shown, the Pistol Lakes are too far south and east, Lower and Upper Unknown are not shown, amongst many other incorrect or missing cartography from the current day. This image is meant only to represent the general travel for the expedition. As Manly Hardy was fond of saying, "Map's wrong."

In the text, Eckstorm refers to Sisladobsissis as Upper Dobsy, and Sisladobsis as Lower Dobsy. The noted Pistol Stream is not depicted, but the tributary branch above Pistol Green might be the best approximation. Spring Lake described in Chapter XXII is not shown on this map, but is north of Lower Pistol Lake. Contrasting these old maps with a more accurate current version makes for an interesting comparison.

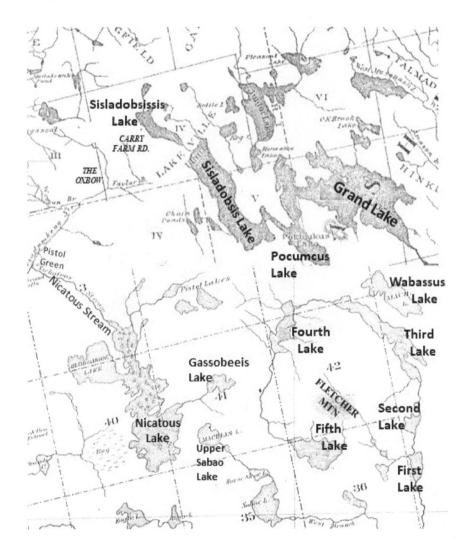

To The Woods
(Editor's Collection)

I — IN TRANSITU

For from toiling town and from sleepy hollow,
We lift our eyes to the hills and pray,
"O, with the wind and the bird to follow
Over the hills and far away!"

from, *Over the Hills and Far Away*
by Anna Boynton Averill

WE ran away this fall. In fleeing the telegraph, the post-office, the door bells, and all our many masters, we experienced a sweet, if guilty satisfaction, which more than compensated the unpropitious skies that followed us, though it was not until we were safe at Nicatowis, where officers of the law no longer go, that we felt quite secure from pursuit and recall. And this is the chronicle of the trip.

We were my father, myself and "Jot."[4] The trip was up the Passadumkeag waters and to the Machias Lakes. Father was guide and head of the expedition. To Jot fell most of the hard work. I wrote the journal and did the admiring. It will be seen that Father and I, by effecting a combination, managed to secure the offices, mine indeed a sinecure, as became my abilities, but his *pro meritis*; for, though Jot knew a large part of the country, Father was easily chief by virtue of the six trips which he had made through it previous to this one. His first was in 1867, when he and Louis Ketchum came up the Machias and found

---

[4] Jot Eldredge. From Manly Hardy's journals, Eldredge traveled with him on this 1890 trip and again in 1899, when accompanied by son Walter Hardy, for Manly's final trip to the woods.

their way across to and down the Passadumkeag without guide or guide book. He had taken the trip twice before with big Sebattis Mitchell, in 1873 and 1874, on the former occasion returning by the St. Croix and the sea, and so up the Penobscot. Once he traveled with Alonzo Spearen; and twice with John Spearen his brother, with whom he made the circuit by way of the Dobsies, Fourth Lake, and Machias Lake to Gassobeeis. In our lenten days on the West Branch last year, when it was uncertain after the kettle had been emptied what would fill it next, Father had told me of the flesh pots[5] of Gassobeeis and Fourth Lake, and even then had planned the trip in expectation of plenty.

We got up at a preposterously early hour one Monday morning, perhaps to balance sitting up so late Saturday night, and took the early train from Bangor. At the Enfield station Gilman's Express was waiting to haul us and our baggage in to Nicatowis, it being shorter, cheaper and easier to haul than it is to work up stream against the current and to carry past Grand and Nicatowis Falls.

It was a superb day, dappled in the early morning and threatening rain, but coming out so fair and fine when once we are on our way that our spirits were light as the breeze. Such blackberries by the roadside, such little brooks — running away, too— hills so inspiring and hollows so delightful— nothing which we saw was passed by unappreciated.

At Wakefield Corner a shoe must be reset, and while we waited, we watched two fish hawks wheeling above the mill pond on the — Escutassis[6] of the maps, Scootahzin of the people.

---

[5] A place providing luxurious living. In Exodus 16:3, King James version, "...in the land of Egypt, when we sat by the flesh pots, and when we did eat bread to the full;..." or in the English Standard version, "...when we sat by the meat pots and ate bread to the full,..."

[6] Near what is now Route 188. Eskutasis Stream passes through the Gristmill Pond, near Burlington.

Annotated Edition

"En route for Nicatous."
(Image courtesy of Special Collections, Raymond H. Fogler Library.)

This photo includes a handwritten caption on the back that reads, "En route for Nicatous." As you will read in Chapter IV, it would be curious if Mrs. Eckstorm actually spelled it that way at the time the photo was taken, or added the caption many years later.

In the photo, two men are at the rear of the wagon resetting the wheel's brake shoe as described in the text. *The Lady Emma,* their trusty canoe, is visible on the tow-wagon.

> Using the high-resolution scan of the photo, and zooming in, the man seated in the buckboard looks to be Manly Hardy. It is well documented that the young Ms. Hardy often carried camera equipment on trips with her father and developed the plates herself.

At Burlington we stopped again, and I dimly remember — do not, in fact, remember, but know it must be true — that a ledge outcrops there which was of slate and shows glacial scratches. I distinctly remember that a gentleman came up, and after examining the canoe critically inquired whether it would hold a man if he didn't put a weight in the bottom. Beyond Burlington we crossed the Madagascal, a beautiful stream, "smart as lightning," Jot said.

From the hilltops further on Spawnook Lake[7] was revealed with Passadumkeag Mountain[8] rising behind it in wooded swells, no finer than as we see it from home lying along the northeast horizon like a long blue cloud, but still very satisfactory. Thence up hill and down and through pine barrens until the main road left us and we passed through the fences of Stickney, the last settler, into the woods road that leads to Nicatowis.

Crossing the Passadumkeag at Grand Falls, and keeping it on our left from this time forward, we came by noon to a little shanty in the midst of a large field. One man stays here to look out for the farm, which is kept up in order to raise supplies for the lumbermen. Here we got dinner, and in the afternoon hauled in to the head of Nicatowis Falls, about four miles beyond, over a road not without stones and stumps, but still good enough for light wagons. At the end of the carry past the falls the load was unpacked and sorted, and all provisions which we thought would not be needed before we returned to this place were hidden in the woods;

---

[7] Now, Saponac Pond.
[8] Passadumkeag Mountain is on the order of 1470 ft. (448 m.).

for it is against father's principles to carry about any unnecessary impedimenta. Then, judging that there was not enough water for all three of us to go up in the canoe, Father and I walked through to the lake while Jot brought up the load.

One does not see much of a lake from the outlet, only a wooded, rocky shore on the right, and on the left a burned point overgrown with bracken and strewn with granite boulders. A few small islands shut off the outward view. At the left of the road by which we reached the lake are the outlet and its dam, newly rebuilt; and also a little house for the use of river drivers and others. The wing of the old dam still extends along the shore for several hundred feet, decayed, broken and growing up to alders, but not needed now that the low land behind has grown up to trees, so that there is no longer any danger of the lake cutting another outlet for itself.

We crossed the dam, which is just at the head of a pretty little rapid where the stream takes a whirl or two among mossy granites before settling quietly into the round pool below, just as Jot arrived with the canoe. The afternoon being now in the decline, we prepared to camp at this place. Though it is true that in the woods one has all the room there is for camping, anyone who knows nothing of this kind of a life, would be astonished to see how hard it sometimes is to find a smooth, dry place large enough to pitch even a small tent. In the present instance we were obliged to pitch ours just below the end of the dam and exactly in the middle of the carry, in an ill-smelling spot, but the best there was.

While Father and Jot were making ready the tent and camp wood, I took up my old occupation of making the bed; and, in the absence of boughs of any kind, cut a great bed of sweet-fern and buckhorn brakes, as the bracken is called here, which partially atoned for the ill savor of the place. In little time, our house keeping arrangements were soon completed.

An empty box which we found nearby was seized on as treasure and became our principal article of furniture. A few blueberries and one little trout, which were all the land and water afforded that night, were laid by toward the next day's needs. As our home luncheon, though small, was no more likely to fail than the widow's meal and oil — *why is it that "store food" always lasts so long in the woods?* — no anxieties for the morrow disturbed our enjoyment of the night, no premonition warned us how we should yet be fed.

II — NICATOWIS RAVENS

"Ah, but I have a grand memory for forgetting."

IT is not often that the event of the day transpires after the blankets have been tucked in. We certainly were all asleep and we must have waked at the same moment, though no one spoke immediately; for at the first word all had agreed that, though very faint, the noise we heard was an awkward bowman rapping his paddle against the gunwale at every stroke. It was most improbable that anyone would be coming down the lake so late at night to camp in the dark; or to walk out seven miles to the Gilman House.

We heard no voices, but when Jot turned out a little after the noise ceased, he found two men walking quietly along the shore end of the dam. They accepted his invitation and came down to the tent.

One was stout and florid with a red, horseshoe moustache and a slouch hat— a very ruddy man. "Ruddy" was spokesman and sat on our box before the fire, his paddle in the hollow of his right arm as he lifted the tent with his left and peered inside to catechise the sleepy.

The other, was slender, brown, and evidently a woodsman. This "Mr. Brown," stood behind the fire, leaning on his paddle as he talked with Jot.

Conversation did not flow at first; we were sleepy and Ruddy seemed distraught. To find strangers encamped in that carry with no possible way of getting past except by the path between the tent and the fire was undeniably awkward. And they were going downstream that night, so they said.

"When did we come and how?" inquired Ruddy.

So we told them how we hauled in with Gilman that day and how near we had been to coming with so-and-so, who was to be in at such a time.

"I know that." Ruddy said with confidence. Straightway he unbent a little. Then he volunteered the information that they had just come from the head of the lake. More questions followed from Ruddy, who seemed inquisitive.

Thereat Father sat up and told all the news, as a good woodsman should; *where this guide was and where that one, who were with them, of the party that had just gone in to Lonz's camp on Pistol,* and all the matters on which he thought our visitors would be already informed; for three to one, a strange woodsman cares less to hear the news, than to know *who you are* that tell these things and whether you tell truth.

"Were we going to Darling's?"

No, we were not out for game.

Ruddy froze at once, and evidently set us down as suspicious characters and possibly as wardens. Again he spoke of going downstream and that they must be going, but made no move himself. Again he put his questions with a delicate indirectness.

The talk wandered to the past, and old experiences, old acquaintances, how places looked ten, twenty, thirty years ago. The fire shining on Ruddy made him redder and cast his shadow on the tent in massive bulk. All the while in the pauses of the talk came his refrain that he never would lug past Nicatowis Falls again, you'd never catch him lugging on that carry again. It was evident that he was as near it as he cared to be that night.

Then said Father plainly, "If you have any meat with you, we would like to buy a few pounds."

"That isn't our business," replied Ruddy briefly and with dignity. After a pause, he asked, "What may your name be?"

"Hardy."

"Of Brewer?"

"Yes."

And then he knew all that he wanted to know.

Having discovered who we were, his frostiness thawed completely. Before they left they told us (what we knew already) that they had no intention of carrying past, but were going to stay at the house at the other side of the dam; that it was not the head of the lake, but the narrows which they had come from; that they had seen something on the shore and shot it as it stood there — a slip of the tongue which another day's acquaintance served to correct; and, finally, that they would be happy to give us all the meat we wanted out of "the prettiest long-eared fellow we ever looked at"— which is calling no names. *Exeunt.*[9]

So the ravens fed us the first day; but the story is intended to teach that the Nicatowis raven is a discerning bird and one which does not drop its bounty before Strangers who come unrecommended.[10]

And the corollary is this: the tale would not now be told if I remembered either the names or the faces of any of the principals of this party; but — so quickly do we forget our benefactors — were we to meet tomorrow I should not be able to identify one of them, not even Brown and Ruddy.

"Ah, man," says Alan Breck,[11] *who might well have been a*

native of Maine, "but I have a grand memory for forgetting."

---

[9] Exeunt – used in a script to mark where certain characters leave the stage.

[10] Ravens are said to lead wolves to carcasses that are too tough for the birds to penetrate with even their sharp beaks. In this way, the two species have a special relationship, although, the ravens are always cautious of feeding in the company of wolves, even if they were the 'finders.' In her reference, Mrs. Eckstorm refers to the Nicatowis poachers as the 'ravens,' for providing them with meat for the start of their journey.

[11] Alan Breck Stewart (1711 – 1791) was a Scottish soldier wrongly accused of the 1752 murder of a royal agent. He inspired the character of the name Alan Breck, the adventurer in the novel, *Kidnapped* by Robert Louis Stevenson.

III — THE DAY OF SMALL THINGS

"These are the events of the day, so few and unimportant that
it seems time lost to chronicle them, and yet of what are most
of our days made up of?"

F. H. E.

THE next day it rained; but as we were up at 4 in the morning, we had a chance before the rain began to see the day break, the white-footed mice that live in the cedar by the "taking out place," the red squirrel which was clipping "cedar buds," as we call the fruit of the arbor vitæ, and all our neighbors save the ravens, who were not early birds.

The white-footed mouse is so strictly nocturnal that although I have felt it hop over me in its nightly explorations through the tent, I had never before seen it alive. It is a dainty little creature, slender in shape, clear gray above and pure white below even to the inner sides of the legs and the underside of its long tail. One which drowned itself in our wash basin last year at Ripogenus measured 7½ inches, of which the tail was 3¾ inches. These had a little house in the heart of the cedar which had been laid open by someone removing a chip, opening a crack just wide enough for them and leaving a little balcony in front of their door. Here they sat gazing at me through the morning dusk like little gray shadows, until they took alarm and scudded up the tree. Apparently, they were living on the cedar buds; but I could not prove it.

The day passed quietly. The men got into their rubber coats and fished, more for occupation than in any hope of success. Father performed his great box-splitting feat to a small but select audience. Jot enticed a colony of shiners which lived under the rocks at the end of the carry to come and nibble his fingers. I wrote up the journal, in which I find it noted that Jot brought me two kinds of everlasting (*G. decurrens and G. polycephalum*),[12] explaining that the former is excellent for colds, while the latter has no medicinal value. It was one of the facts which are often of prime importance to the woodsman. Rock polypod, we learned later, is good for diarrhea; yellow ash bark to produce sweating; and Father once saved his own life by compounding a medicine of pine bark, the inner bark of wild cherry and lungwort (the rough lichen which grows on swamp maples), steeped together and sweetened with honey. I myself can testify to the many virtues and the bad taste of the last compound.

Trout were not abundant at the dam and, though the place was faithfully fished both up stream and down, only three were caught for the day. The largest of these, a fine 14-inch fish, was given us by our ravens whose kindness is remembered even though their names are not. In the afternoon two salmon about 11 and 14 inches in length took their fly and a large one broke their rigging. These differed in color from all the young salmon I had ever seen, being of a fine green bronze with silvery bellies and with dark, almost black, spots on the sides, so mottled that at a little distance they resembled mackerel more than trout. Salmon appear to be abundant in Nicatowis, whether sea salmon or landlocked I do not know, though I am informed that the sea salmon introduced by the Game Commissioners have become land locked, refusing to migrate. While Father was fishing just above the sluice a great blue heron lighted on the gate not 10 feet away, looking "for all the world," so those who saw him say, like a great mosquito as he settled with long legs outstretched and his neck bent down almost between them.

---

[12] Gnaphalium polycephalum is a genus of flowering plants in the sunflower family. Commonly called "cudweeds."

These are the events of the day, so few and unimportant that it seems time lost to chronicle them, and yet of what are most of our days made up of?

We had pleasant company; enough to eat of the best there was, though it was given us; more to see than ordinarily falls into one day's limits, for besides the mice, squirrels, shiners, trout, salmon and heron, various small birds sought the tent and gossiped with us — chickadees, Maryland yellow-throats and a beautiful black and white creeper.

The place was pretty, too, with the tall pine and big, mossy granites behind, the carry path fringed with alders leading down to the pool and clear sky over the hill in front. It being our first camp on this trip, it had moreover, pleasant associations for Father, who, sixteen years or more ago, cut out the present carry, shortening the old carrying place by about one-half and thereby benefitting all who have followed.

With all these aids to contentment, and with minds that were free from worries for a time and willing to rest from labor, it is no wonder that the time passed pleasantly. If the next one who goes there finds it forlorn and uncomfortable, sees nothing praiseworthy, that, too, need not be wondered at; for it is the small things which make the difference in our days.

Appreciation Of The Small Things
(Editor's Collection)

IV — NICATOWIS

"I have been set down as a notorious poacher and outlaw, but really I am more of a poacher than an outlaw, and more so in the papers than otherwise."

Jock Darling

EVERYBODY knows where Nicatowis is, how to reach it, and what he can get when he is there; but why is it that so few know how to spell it? It is Nicatowis, not Nicatous, nor Nickertous — as may easily be demonstrated. Nicatow, in Indian, is the fork, and primarily the junction of the east and west branches of the Penobscot at Medway, which itself was formerly called Nicatow.

Nicatowis is the diminutive — the Little Fork. It was formerly applied to the confluence of the main stream Passadumkeag and what is now called the Nicatowis Branch. The lake above was Giassobee, or Clear Water Lake, into which flowed Giassobee*sis* — Little Clear Water Lake — now corrupted into Gassobeeis. This latter name is evidence on its face that a larger lake of the same system, which could have been nothing but the present Nicatowis, must have been called Giassobee, for *is* or *sis* is strictly a comparative term, exactly equivalent to *lesser*. So that not only is Nicatowis a misnomer in its root meaning, but we can prove that another name must necessarily have been applied to the lake, which name was Giassobee. It is now too late to correct the error in names, but the spelling should be reformed to Nicatowis, which is good Indian and represents the correct pronunciation.

Not that hundreds of people do not say Nicatous, but they mean to use the other form. A clear cut and elegant pronunciation is not characteristic of Maine people; they clip and slur their words whenever possible. Strangers usually make too hard work of their Indian, like the one who called Mattawamkeag, Matwampsumpkehac; the native-born soften Passadumkeag to Parsydunky or even to Parsdunky. Olamon becomes Old Lemon; Nesowadnehunk, Sourdyhunk; Chesuncook is Suncook, and Caucomgomocsis, familiarly known as "The Sis."

No wonder there is difficulty in deciding the proper form. Again, sometimes three or four names for the same place are in current use, as Little Telos Lake, which is called Telosilos, Telosinis and Tellisannis, as well as Pataquongamis and Round Pond. Abol also is known by four or five different names. There is no standard authority for either spelling or pronunciation.

The State maps and reports are hopelessly incorrect. The pronunciation of the people is hard to catch and often corrupt or abbreviated beyond recognition. Most of the Indians themselves do not know what the names mean. Even most of the well-intentioned people who have tried to help us out of the mud have only made matters worse by becoming mired themselves. The notable exceptions have been Thoreau and Mr. Hubbard, who have probably done more than all others taken together to give permanence to some of our Indian names and secure for these a uniform orthography.[13]

Yet, now and then, though rarely, an error has crept past even their vigilance. For example, to the rounded hill with one sheer side which

---

[13] Eckstorm had a wide appreciation for the work of Thoreau, a topic which will be covered more fully in the appendix of this book. Hubbard, an explorer and writer who may not be as familiar to many, spent more time than Thoreau on correctly identifying the proper Indian place names in northern Maine. Hubbard's work is documented in his 1884 book, "Woods and Lakes of Maine. A Trip from Moosehead Lake to New Brunswick in a Birch-Bark Canoe." The second subtitle of his book was, "To which are added some Indian place-names and their meanings."

rises above the wooded level east of Chesuncook, Mr. Hubbard gives the name Sowbunge Mountain, probably copying, and undoubtedly copying correctly, the form given by some lumberman or hunter; but where in Sowbunge does one find the beauty and the elegance of the original Sowangawas, the Eagle's Nest? Who shall say what Mattagoodus and Pattygumpus once were, or whether there ever was any poetry in Crosshuntic?

For sins of ignorance and sins of omission no doubt there is pardon; but what shall be said of people who deliberately rename us; who come on trips of exploration, and, going home, announce themselves the discoverers of lakes which were lumbered and hunted on before they were born? Who, perceiving that our ponds are lakes, wrench away the name which some pioneer had left to the pond of his choice as his only memorial, to dub it Echo Lake, or Eagle Lake, or Green Lake?

Aren't there enough such prosy names in the world already without prosy people being allowed to make more of them? Better Shin Pond, Tumble-down-Dick, Pollywog and Poke-Moonshine to the end of their days than to be added to the list of Echo Lakes, Long Lakes and Mud Ponds,[14] which already exceeds in length the line of Banquo's progeny.[15]

Two names, supplanted by accident it may be, should be restored in the next edition of Hubbard's map. Both lie in Seven in Fifteen — Rowe Pond of the map, which is Ross's Pond, named for John Ross, the Bangor lumberman; and Poland Pond so called, which is by good rights Island Pond, as the large island in it shows.

---

[14] There are over sixty known ponds by the name of Mud in Maine.

[15] The witches prediction in Macbeth that Banquo will be the progenitor of kings.

Annotated Edition

Maine Townships and Ranges

By "Seven in Fifteen," Eckstorm is referring to the T.R. mapping. Tp. VII, R. XV stands for township seven, in region fifteen. R is the range number counted from the easterly line to the west.

T.VII, R.XV (T7 R15) is (mostly) north of Caucomgomoc Lake and (somewhat) southeast of Allagash Lake. It is a curious thing, why Eckstorm picked on these two lakes with name errors on Hubbard's map, of which there were plenty of disputes at the time. But then again, it is not, as we shall see why.

In the fall of 1859, her father, Manly, and trapping partner Rufus Philbrook, built a hunting camp in the region near Caucomgomoc Lake. During that trip, we know the two trappers bagged 75 muskrat, approx. 50 sable, 35 mink, 7 beaver, 4 black bear, 4 fisher, 3 lynx, and 2 otter. Such are the details kept by Manly Hardy in his journals.

It is thus with assuredness, and knowing the penchant for correctness in these things of the woods that ran in the Hardy family, that it was likely Mr. Hardy who took first exception to these two ponds, as so named, on the Hubbard map. Especially considering Mr. Hardy's association with this area of the north woods during his time trapping.

An image from Hubbard's 1899 edition of his map shows, eight years following the article from Mrs. Eckstorm, the map was not revised in these two instances.

Hubbard had also labeled Poland Pond with the corresponding Indian name, Kwānä'tacongōmah'so, a technique he usually applied.

I cannot imagine there was any animosity between Manly or Fannie Hardy Eckstorm, and Lucius Hubbard over the names placed on the map, as their correspondence over the years shows nothing but respect and admiration for one another in a very professional relationship.

(Reference Maine Gazetteer map 55)

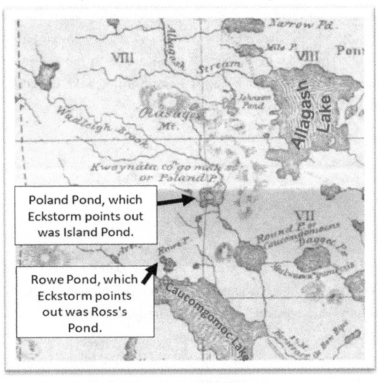

from Hubbard's 1899 Map

The Sapompkeag of the map is the Napompkeag of the white hunters, but the Indians call it Labombic and say that it means rope. These are most likely printers' errors and excusable; but when it comes to malicious rechristening — why, how would you feel if your name were St. Vincent and a stranger told you that it was Robinson, or if not that it ought to be, and he would see to it that you came when he called you?

In a country where all communication must be by water, those places are most important which command the routes between the most rivers.

Nicatowis does this preeminently. From it, by short carries, one may reach Brandy Pond on the head of Union River; the Sabao Lakes on the West Machias; and, by way of Gassobeeis, the Middle Machias Lakes; and through these the St. Croix waters are easily accessible. Nicatowis is also not far distant from the head of the Narraguagus. Thus, it is the highway to all the principal canoeing waters in eastern Maine. Chamberlain Lake in the north and Nicatowis in the east are the two strong points in the Maine woods — and Darling holds the latter, not by accident let us believe.

Annotated Edition

Jock Darling

This is the second mention of the name Darling by the writer. The first was with the encounter in Chapter II with the "ravens," when "Ruddy" and "Brown," asked if the Hardys and Jot were on their way to "Darling's."

Jonathan "Jock" Darling was born in Enfield, Maine, on September 28, 1830. His family farmed and hunted the land to earn a sustenance living. As a teen, Darling worked as a cook's helper in a logging camp and tended trap lines. By the time he was around twenty years of age he was a skilled hunter and trapper, who preferred to hunt alone.

In a paper written by James Vickery,[16] he notes that Darling, "between the decades of 1850 and 1880, had claimed to have killed over 1,500 moose and hundreds of deer and caribou." Darling sold the

---

[16] James B. Vickery III, "Jock Darling: The Notorious "Outlaw" of the Maine Woods." Maine History, Vol. 41, No. 3 (2002). *Compiled by Richard W. Judd.*

hides and shipped the meat to markets. This was a time in Maine history when game was severely being over-hunted. The sparse game laws, and little means to enforce those that were enacted, led to an attitude of, "If I don't take what I can, someone else will." The topic was covered brilliantly by Fannie Hardy in a series in *Forest and Stream* in 1891. As early as 1874, John Way, Jr., in *"Guide to Moosehead Lake, and Northern Maine."* devoted a third of the book to voluntary conservation measures across the globe as a plea to the Maine hunter.[17]

Darling quickly developed a reputation as someone to steer clear of, and a person that took revenge. One story widely told, tells of when he was accused of not paying his room and board bill and ejected from a lumber camp at Nicatous. On taking his leave, Jock is said to have 'shot up the camp,' and it was suspected that in the middle of the night, he stole all the chains for the teamsters sleds, effectively shutting down the lumber camp operations.

Darling was hunting and trapping long before there were Game Laws in Maine. The first laws, which were difficult to enforce, began to be written around the end of the 1860s. Darling was like many who hunted the woods of Maine at the time for game, either to eat or sell; these hunters were often accused of not following the laws. With hunting and fishing becoming big tourist business for Maine, the sporting camp owners, who serviced 'sports' from away, began petitioning the Game Commission for stricter laws and enforcement against native poachers in order to preserve the game population for their client's experiences in the woods.

---

[17] For a summary of John Way's book with excerpts, see, "Thomas S. Steele's Maine Adventures," by Tommy Carbone, Two Book Collection, Burnt Jacket Publishing, 2021.

To take advantage of the business opportunity, Darling had taken to guide work and in the 1870s he built his first hunting lodge at Nicatous Lake. This is *"The Darling's"* referred to in this book. He later opened a second camp on Grand Lake Sebois.

The most famous of encounters for Darling came from his clashes with the State of Maine Game Commission and Game Wardens. Not only was he a notorious poacher, he hunted deer with his dogs which was against the law, a law he vehemently disagreed with.

In an unusual turn of events, Darling took a position as a Maine Game Warden. Shortly after, he wrote a letter to a local paper stated his motivations for protecting fish and game were aligned with his beliefs, and as a sporting lodge owner, he had a duty to his clients to protect the game.

Meanwhile, in a letter to *Forest and Stream*, he had stated his misgivings as a warden for arresting someone who had, "killed for meat when he was hungry." This attitude was common in Maine amongst many landowners and farmers, once a close season was instituted for game; game they had hunted for generations to feed their families. Darling's continued use of dogs for hunting deer led to continued friction with the Game Commissioner.

In a much-debated and publicized story, which will not be covered in detail here, it appears that the Game Commission set up Darling. They hired a Boston detective, McNamara, to pose as a 'sport,' and to hire Darling as a guide. On a Sunday (a day hunting was not permitted) in 1889, Darling's dogs were used to chase deer and the detective shot the deer.

Darling was arrested by McNamara the following week, serving a warrant that Jock was not permitted to read at the time, but charged him with taking a bribe and not upholding the Fish and Game Laws under his sworn duty as a warden.

For eight long years, Darling fought the charges. Ultimately, in January 1897, the case was dismissed.

Jock Darling died the following January of 1898.

The following comments from the *Forest and Stream* issue of January 15, 1898 are illustrative of the times and Darling:

Jan. 8. — Jonathan Darling, well known to sportsmen as "Jock," died at his home in Lowell, Me., on Wednesday, Jan. 5, after an illness of nearly two years. He was sixty-eight years of age and one of the pioneers in the business of entertaining sportsmen from out of the State. He built his famous camps at Nicatous Lake over twenty years ago, and many sportsmen will be pained to learn of his death.

An excellent guide and a thorough woodsman, he was beloved by those he took charge of. He always believed in his right to hunt game as he chose, and his remarkable defense of himself at the time he was under a cloud for breaking the game laws was widely published. He visited the office of the Forest and Stream *and other papers, taking great interest in hunting and fishing matters, and always inspired editors and writers as a man of integrity, though possibly mistaken as to his rights.*

He even became a game warden afterward, so great was the confidence of the Maine Commissioners in his ability and integrity, could he be brought to sec matters in their true light. But he was afterward removed, not wholly converted to the new ideas of fish and game protection. He was always looked up to as an authority on fish and game questions, especially in regard to the numbers of moose, caribou and deer. The many sportsmen he has guided from this section speak in the kindest terms of his skill as a guide and woodsman, of his integrity in all matters pertaining to a guide and camp-keeper.

Forest and Stream also re-published these earlier autobiographical comments from Darling himself:

I was quick to learn the habits and nature of the wild animals, and, being good with the gun and not easily excited, I soon got to be quite successful. I kept improving, and as years rolled on I began to hunt for the Boston market. This was some forty-five years ago. Then I could kill moose near home, where I could drive to them with a team. Later on I hunted moose for their hides. I did not believe this was right, but the Indians and many white hunters made a business of it and I saw that they were sure to kill them all, and so I took a hand in it. and have killed over a hundred in a year, until they were nearly exterminated. I never killed any caribou or deer for their hides, but piles of them for the markets.

I have been set down as a notorious poacher and outlaw, but really I am more of a poacher than an outlaw, and more so in the papers than otherwise. I have advocated the use of dogs to hunt deer on bare ground and to drive them to water, and have used them in violation of our law, for which readers of Forest and Stream have made a great deal of trouble for me. Now I have accepted the office of Fish and Game Warden, and am confident that I can do good in the cause of game protection.

The dog in the stern of the canoe is the dog Tinker, that the wardens made so much talk about at my lawsuit with them. As I have been such a notorious outlaw, etc. I did not know but you would wish to show your readers what a bad looking creature I am.

J. Darling.

Jock and His Dog, Tinker.
(Photo in *Forest and Stream*, January 1898.)

Jonathan "Jock" Darling
(Photo courtesy the, *Fannie Hardy Eckstorm Collection*, University of Maine,
Special Collections.)

But Nicatowis itself, though the principal feeder of the Passadumkeag, is on the shorter of the two branches. The other, known as the Main Stream, wanders down a general southwesterly course through broad meadows, rising in ponds, but principally dependent upon its brooks — Brown, the two Taylors, Wyman and others[18] — until it receives the Nicatowis Branch at the Fork about twelve miles below the lake, thence it flows westerly, still through low land and meadows, enlarged by the tribute of the two Lord Brooks, the Mattagascal, Scootahzin and Cold Stream. It is a placid course, little broken by rapids and only once expanding into a lake, emptying into the Penobscot about thirty-five miles above Bangor.

Last year when Darling was arrested, several newspapers published the statement that Nicatowis is "fifty miles from the nearest railroad station, and to reach it one must travel over a rough road." Without attempting to state the actual distance, it may be said that we hauled from Enfield to the Gilman House, seven miles from the lake, in four hours and a half, including stops, and the road was as good as any of equal length in eastern Maine. Those who gave the information may take either horn of the dilemma on which they prefer to hang themselves, but these are the facts: it is not a very long nor a very hard day's walk to go from the railroad to Nicatowis.

Though neither a handsome nor an ugly lake, the friends of Nicatowis are safe when they praise its good looks. It has features, and some lakes have none. It is a wooded lake, surrounded by low swells which nowhere approach the dignity of mountains; very irregular in shape, indented with long points and further broken by islands; bounded by hard shores, which, though sheer and without sunken rocks, are nevertheless forbidding to the canoeman and afford camping places only where interrupted by some little beach of gravel or disintegrated granite. It is a

---

[18] North of Pistol Green.

granite lake — shores of loose granite, ledges of granite, islands with solid foundations of the best of granite, and a back country full of it. Now granite never has any suggestions of soft corners and cosiness; it is rugged and downright — real New England stuff. On the other hand, it always presents a tidy appearance. It may be because granite abounds that the first impression of Nicatowis upon a stranger is that it is rough but clean.

Of its irregularity nothing need be said, for such matters are not made clearer by description. For one item, two sets of narrows divide it into three parts of almost equal length, and these are further subdivided by points into bays and coves, one of which, West Lake, is recognized by a name of its own, while others, like Duck Cove, though smaller, are still of considerable extent. When we went up the lake, I attempted to map it, and succeeded fairly well in getting in most of the islands and curves as far as Norway Point, by aid of all the information I could extract from the others as to which were islands and what main land and what was out of sight.

When from Darling's we saw the lake spread out with all its bays and islands, and knew that there was much more unrevealed, my map terminated suddenly with the remark:

"And so on, to infinity."

Annotated Edition

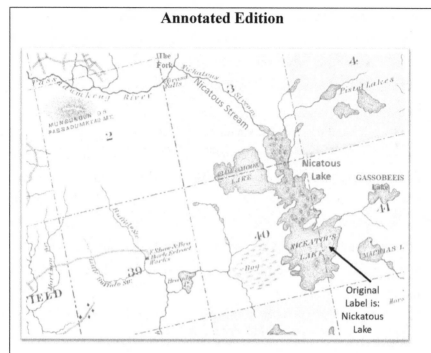

Map Detail of Nicatous Stream and Lake

Nicatous Lake is the second largest lake in Hancock County, at 8 miles long, 5,165 acres, and a max depth of 56 feet. The map image is based on maps of Hancock County, Maine from around the 1870s.

Notice the original labeling on this map as "Nickatous," with a k. This is a spelling variant even Fannie Hardy had not covered at the beginning of the chapter. Gassobeeis was not labeled on the original and the Pistols are depicted too far to the east and south.

V — "TO GASSOBEEIS AND CAMPED."

*"The loon is the spirit of the lake. To hear the loon's cry at
night is almost as if the lake were speaking."*
in, *The Bird Book*
by Fannie Hardy Eckstorm

WHEN we started Wednesday morning the loons were flying overhead,
which we usually account a sign of wind, but we made the run to
Darling's with only a light breeze following. We stopped there a moment
for old acquaintance sake, but, as Mr. Darling was in Lowell, stayed only
long enough to get a view of the lake and to look at the establishment
which has been built since father was there last. It seems superfluous to
write any description of Darling's — a log house of one room, a lean-to
and a loft; situated on a rocky promontory running out between West
Lake and the main Nicatowis; clean and comfortable within, and well
supplied with tables and benches; but we greatly admired the strong
strategic value of the place and in the selection recognized Darling's
well-known astuteness. Surrounded on three sides by water it commands
an extensive view of every avenue of approach by water, while on the
fourth side a cleared field, extending back many rods, is well defended,
if one can judge from the lay of the land, by thick and tangled woods,
difficult to penetrate.

Gassobeeis Stream, for which we were heading, lies about east from
Darling's behind the long point which runs out from the east shore,
forming part of the upper narrows. The stream is usually rather shallow,
so that in several places the passengers commonly have to get out and

"farm it" while the guide "waits on her," to use technical terms. But this year the water was high and had been raised artificially by putting in two little dams which flowed out part of the rapids. One of these caused no trouble, but concerning the other there is a tale.

Father is better than a guidebook to tell you in advance what you are coming to, for he never forgets a place once having seen it, and he knows Gassobeeis Stream perfectly, every rock and turn in it. Accordingly, before we reached the place, he told us of some shoal water ahead, past which he and I must walk. There was a steep bank at the lower end of the carry, he said, and at its head an old dam with a sluiceway built high for gates. Below it was a hollow log which Sebattis used to call his cannon. We came to the foot of the quick water. The bank was there with a path running up it through plenty of buckhorn brakes nearly waist high and as wet as rain could make them. We went up the hill and down it, and then the carry dived under water for a space. Father was amazed; that carry never had been flowed in his day. Then I told him that from the top of the hill I had seen a small dam just round the turn below which we got out.

"But the dam was not there," objected he, as willing to believe that the water was running up hill as that he was mistaken.

Nevertheless, a dam I had seen, and this was the flowage of it. So we struck out for the stream, through "squaw bush" (*Cornus stolonifera*),[19] alders and blue joint grass, all very wet and sufficiently thick, got loganned,[20] backed out and tried again, found a place at last where, by

---

[19] The American Dogwood or Red Stem Dogwood.

[20] The Indian word *pokelogan* was interpreted by Thoreau as an inlet that led nowhere. *Logan* is a shortened form and used several times in this book. It means a shallow place. The meaning is similar to the word, *logon*, used

venturing on some old, slimy, and presumably rotten, sticks, I got across dry-footed and he with one boot full of water; at last got to the canoe again, Father still insisting that the place wasn't natural. Soon we met bubbles floating down.

"That means quick water," said he, "but there can't be any above this, for the dam is the head of things."

Then, suddenly, round a turn, as if to speak for itself, up rose the old dam, shining and black as of yore, with the water running through the old sluiceway and Sebattis's "cannon" still there. The dam below, which Father had not seen at all, was one of the temporary affairs, and as Jot and I were both strangers to the place our testimony had not served for his enlightenment.

Gassobeeis is pretty as such streams go. All navigable streams are apt to be disappointing to those whose ideas are drawn entirely from pictures and their own fancies, who look for noble forests free from underbrush, traversed by clear streams with gravelly beds on which lie,

> "silver scalit fishes
> With fynnys schynand broun as synopar
> And chyssell talys."[21]

---

by Hubbard. Eckstorm was consulted by W.F. Ganong for his publication, "An organization of the scientific investigation of the Indian place nomenclature of the Maritime Provinces of Canada," (1914). She told him of how, "lumbermen speak of 'loganning' logs, when they store them in logans."

[21] This is the first of two times in the writing where Eckstorm quotes from Gavin Douglas. Douglas was a Scottish bishop, royal court poet, and translator. One of his greatest achievements was his 1513 work *Eneados*, a translation of the Æneid into Scots. This partially quoted passage is from the Twelfth Prologue, which celebrates the beauty of Nature.

Such are seldom met in real life. Real streams are apt to run through meadows, bogs or flowed land; or if otherwise it is usually the worse for the canoeman. Their banks are thick with alders and scrub growth; were it not so that would be the worse for the hunter. And their dark waters suggest bullfrogs and mud turtles, instead of the red-finned trout which actually inhabit them.

The lower part of Gassobeeis Stream runs through alder ground and birches; the upper part is a bog brook and must have been a famous beaver country in the old days. Lambkill, sweet gale, leather-leaf, rhodora and all the heaths grow in abundance along the banks giving a soft and pleasant tone to the landscape. I like bogs; they are very restful to look at, and always mean "plain sailing."

When we reached Gassobeeis Lake we found that Father's old camp ground among the Norways on the left had been burned over, and the rain recommencing, we were forced to take the first spot available. Yet not even camping in the rain is a hardship; it only makes work more the livelier. All help in unloading and covering the goods, one looks for the ridgepole, one for the crotches, tent pins are cut from the nearest bush and in how short a time the tent is up. No matter if it is damp at first, it soon dries. And the water shakes off the boughs so thoroughly that the bed is not very damp. It is one of Father's fancies always to have some splits of cedar or a piece of spruce bark or canvas to lay down along the sides of the tent for the double purpose of preventing small articles being lost and keeping the camp stuff dry. We always carry something of the kind in the canoe with us, abandoning it only when we come to a carry. He also leaves on the back tent-pole an inch or two of the side limbs, which make strong and convenient hooks for hanging clothing and guns.

We carry as little baggage as we can and then always have too much. The tent and blankets, a firkin for small groceries and a box for flour and bacon, cooking utensils and clothing make up considerably more than the bulk of the outfit. There is no room in one canoe for three people and the luxuries of camping out. If by these one understands folding campstools and rubber air beds, adjustable tables and patent camp stoves, frying-pans with hinged handles and all the other folding and unfolding nuisances which are advertised to make miserable the lives of sportsmen.

Place your load with a two-mile carry always in mind, and there's many an indispensable will stay at home in the corner without being missed When the books and opera glasses and sun umbrellas begin to appear, the old stager knows you are green and pities your guide.

Don't take too many clothes. You are persuaded into it in the vain belief that you will want to change now and then, or that when you come out you will want to put on something different from the clothes you have worn and slept in for a month. It is a delusion. Cleanliness is no more natural to the uncivilized man than godliness. You will find that you can always pick out the guide because he is the best dressed man in the party; and, on the other score, after four weeks' jaunting in a rubber bag, your best suit might very well be mistaken for your worst. In either case, all you have on smells of smoke and fir boughs, and will smell of it for weeks to come, though you may be unconscious, so that you need not suppose that your fellow travelers do not know where you have been.

If you take extra clothing on chances of getting wet, the chances are ten to nothing that if you are wet enough to shift, it will be by a general capsize and your spare clothes will be as wet as the others; or you may be drowned and so not need them after all. But if you persist in carrying what you do not want, don't take old ones. "The woods is the worst place in the world to wear out old clothes," say the hunters. For myself I shall never again take an extra dress. With a short skirt for the woods and a long one for occasions, a woman can go into the woods and return as far as Bangor in safety, if not without shame. I have tried it.

We do not carry any canned provisions except condensed milk. They are heavy and inconvenient to pack, and we would rather have simpler fare and fewer turns on the carries. Flour and potatoes will preserve life, and the Spartan discipline of being obliged to procure your luxuries or go without them, adds flavor to them. Father declares that when his pole and gun will not supply him something with bones in it, he will no longer go in the woods. So far, for the first day or two, we never have failed at a single meal to have meat or fish of some kind in the kettle; though sometimes thrift has caused the remnants or the supper to coldly furnish forth the breakfast table. But we are not too proud to accept a gift, which helps out sometimes.

ANNOTATED EDITION

The North Woods and Anna Boynton Averill

In the *Forest and Stream* issue, on the pages following Mrs. Eckstorm's article, the following submission from J. F. Sprague of Monson, Maine is printed. The north woods region Sprague describes is the subject of the books by Lucius L. Hubbard, and the area mentioned by Eckstorm in this book.

At the conclusion of his article, Sprague included the poem *Northern Maine*, by Anna Boynton Averill (1843 – 1915). Averill, was an accomplished poet, who published a large collection of her poems in the book, "Birch Stream And Other Poems," (1908). She was born in Alton, Maine, and as of the 1870 census was employed as a teacher and living in Dover of Piscataquis County.

ANGLING RETREATS OF MAINE

Forest and Stream
January 22, 1891

GENERALLY, those who have written about the Maine forests, streams, lakes, ponds and softly-running brooks have been visitors from abroad and not residents of our own Pine Tree State.

In attempting to inform the readers of *Forest and Stream* of the certain retreats in the woods of Maine, where large numbers have and many more may enjoy the pleasures of camp life, trout and landlocked salmon fishing, and the shooting of large and small game, I have no apology to offer. Being a near resident to the places and scenes which I shall attempt to describe "I Know whereof I affirm," and I hope these lines may lead others to these green and sylvan woods, grand old mountains and charming ponds, lakes and rivers, there to enjoy the delights which I have myself experienced.

The immense throng of city denizens who are vacationists for weeks and months, and who are devoted followers in their annual pilgrimages of Peter the Apostle and the sainted Walton, are assuredly multiplying in the American nation. Many seek the seashore and yet numberless others the mountains and quiet nooks of the hill country. Others are charmed by green fields, clear skies and fine scenery, but all of them are fascinated by the alluring trout and gamy salmon in the remote forest lakes, around which dwell the fleet deer and where the moose has his own abiding place.

Owing to the fact that more than one-half of the area of the State of Maine is yet covered with a verdant forestry, that one-tenth of its broad domain is inland water ways; that its vast forests are inhabited by the game of primitive times, and its waters by the fish of the aboriginals, and that nature has fashioned within our realm some of the grandest scenery in the world, we are rapidly becoming the summer home for countless dwellers in the great marts of the republic.

In all of northern Maine there is no portion that is more entirely a beautiful lake country than is the north western part of Piscataquis county. Within a radius of ten miles of Monson are some thirty or more lakes and ponds where spotted and lake trout are abundant.

Here the tourist can select just such an outing as his health will permit or his tastes and inclinations may dictate. He can tarry at a modern and well-appointed hotel and drive over pleasant country roads, feasting his eyes upon delightful landscapes, to a different trout pond each day for weeks, or he can penetrate the lone wilderness and camp beside the still waters in nature's own lodges and repose upon cedar "twigs" and spruce branches under aged forest trees, amid the

> *Music of birds and rustling of young boughs,*
> *And sound of swaying branches and the voice*
> *Of distant waterfalls.*

It is occasionally suggested by visitors and strangers that we who are domiciled amid all this wealth of grandeur and wild beauty, among these lakes of trout and near the stealthy retreats of the moose, deer and bear, do not entertain a just appreciation of what has been so lavishly bestowed upon us. But this is, I believe, an imputation without foundation. From the rough old hunter and weather-beaten trapper, whose homes are among the spruce trees, to the more favored sons and daughters who are "to the manner born" all have an abiding love for the mountains, lakes and forests.

As evidence of this I cite the following lines from the pen of a Piscataquis writer of some note, Anna Boynton Averill.

Northern Maine

My native wilds! for years untold,
The morning touched your hills with gold,
The north wind swept your fragrant glooms,
And bore the larch and pine perfumes
Across your lakes of lily blooms.

The fir, the hemlock and the pine
Sang on the heights; — and moss and vine
Made many a far, dim valley sweet
And shadowy for the shy fawn's feet.

In silvery solitudes the loon
Laughed with the echoes; and the moon
Made splendor on the mountains when
The Storm King slept, unseen of men.

O woods, and lakes, and wandering streams!
Ye have awakened from your dreams.
Your sweet breath blew abroad. Beware!
The gay world comes and finds you fair.

— Will all wild things take wing away?
I ween I would an' I were they,
Up these deep waterways I'd fare
If I were wolf, or moose, or bear,
Or bird, or fawn, or fox, or hare!

O Northern wilds! you surely hold
In your great heart some refuge old,
Safe hid and far and deep and dumb,
Where the gay world will never come!

Northern Maine Pond
(Editor's Collection)

VI — LAKE OF PLEASANT MEMORIES

"Ahwassus, the Bear — Huge and round he was, like the beast he was named for, but strong and wise, and in his dark, flat face and small, twinkling eyes there were resources, ambitions, schemes."

in, *The Penobscot Man*
by Fannie Hardy Eckstorm

GASSOBEEIS is a lovely lake. High land compasses it. On one side the hills rise toward Sabas. In the north, Duck Lake Mountain shows a changing side, green or blue, mellowed into purple by the sunset. The lake itself is rather more than two miles long by a mile in width, surrounded by hard, dry shores, free from dead wood, green and inviting. Near the shores the water is shoal, and the ice, forming on it in past ages, has taken up all the large rocks save a very few and carried them into the sea-wall on the shore, leaving the bottom hard and clean. In this shallow water, especially near the outlet, the lake is grown up to rushes and water lilies, the former dressing it till it looks like a grass field, the latter in their season making it a parterre of hundreds of acres of the loveliest blossoms. Trout are the fish here. The only pickerel which I ever heard to be caught was so maimed and deformed that it was probably dropped here by some fish hawk flying over from Fourth Lake. Gassobeeis is a paradise for small game; all wild things seem to love it. The ducks sail off among the rushes conversing with each other, the deer wade out into the shallows to feed and escape the flies, and the bears follow the shores for cranberries and huckleberries in their season.

Here, Father had a camping place just to his mind. Many pleasant memories clustered about it, and whether he thought of it in summer or winter it was always home — home and a quiet haven after stormy Nicatowis, home and a clean caravansary after the slime and desolation of Fourth Lake. Here they could get all the ducks they wanted and trout from the pool on the stream, or venison if they wished it. Here, after the blankets were spread down after supper and the fire built up for the night, Big Sebattis used to repeat that story whose repetition never wearies, the old "Sung um joyfully," always preluding the tale with the query, "Never we told it you that time how she sung it 'Joyfully' Old Isaac?"

Annotated Edition

Big Sebattis Mitchell

Photograph from the collection of Fannie Hardy Eckstorm. Her handwritten caption reads, "Big Sebattis Mitchell - taken 1891." Mitchell, a woodsman and lumberman, two skills more often not found in one man, is a prominent character in Eckstorm's, "The Penobscot Man."

(Image courtesy of Special Collections, Raymond H. Fogler Library.)

Gassobeeis seems to belong to Sebattis more than to anyone else. He, too, loved it well. He enjoyed the *"great deal scenery"* and the good living, and he often expressed the wish to Father that their wives might be there to share it — *"our women,"* as he used to put it with an air of pride and ownership. He frequently told the story of his courtship, dwelling with satisfaction on the times when he *"was great deal favor with old folks, specially young ones."* He was a man of fine sensibilities despite the two hundred and sixty odd pounds of flesh which obscured the inner light to strangers, alive to beauty, exquisitely humorous, softer-hearted than even the generality of woodsmen. "These hard hearts," of which Lear complains, find few hiding places in the woods; is there a cure in nature for them?

Sebattis would not indulge in even the brutality of kindness when the kindness could only save his own feelings. *"We cut you t'roat tomor' mornin',"* he said to the baby seal that must starve for lack of milk, but for the sight he fondled it and made it happy. He was a consummate raconteur. With how much pathos he told the story of the death of little Johnny. With what appreciation he described the man to whom he sold the blackfish oil, so that Justice herself seemed to wink at their deceiving such a judge of oil. A literary instinct guided him to the telling points of his narrative, and he grasped them with a firm hand; repetition he used when effective, but never the aimless retrogressions of the ignorant and unskilled; when he digressed, it was to express some quaint, original thought or call up some philosophical question. He never doubted that his stories were worth hearing and he never apologized for their length. He was a master of the use of details and had to tell long stories. He never quarreled with his genius nor cropped the tail of his Pegasus. If his audience got to sleep under a double number he reproachfully asked, *"What for you gone sleep? Why you don' gone wake?"* and began again at the point where he judged the thread had been broken. Hunting stories, his trials as governor, old legends, stories of porpoise shooting at

Quoddy and tales of the sea were in his repertory. And all began alike with, "*Never we told it you that time when —*" as if all had been many times rehearsed to different audiences. Ahwassus, the Bear, the other Indians have nicknamed him. He says that bears can talk, but won't. He always talks to them when he meets them, calls them cowards, says they understand Indian because they look ashamed. Brother to brother it must be when they meet— the Indians were right in calling him *Ahwassus*, the Bear; each big, and fat, and strong, with brown faces and little eyes, strong sense and sagacity. It was Gasaobeeis that revealed thee, O Sebattis Wassus.

We got two ducks and some berries while at Gassobeeis this time, but nothing else except a box. Ducks were not abundant here this year. Toward evening we heard in the west a strange, rumbling noise, not thunder— the sky was clear — a distant, low-pitched sound that seemed as much in the earth as in the air. The others said it sounded like rolling logs from a brow landing, but I could liken it to nothing except the noise in Lorna Doone,[22] which rose from the moors at eventide and died away in wailing.

In the morning, after the fog cleared, we made ready to go to Machias. True to his principles, never to lug an extra pound, Father began his preparations by sorting out all that we could leave behind. Even from our load there was a considerable pile laid aside to be hidden — all our spare clothes, except boots and stockings, for one thing, and our best hats, which were stored under the box found the day before.

We took with us only the necessaries of life, and as few of them as possible. This translated to only a week's rations of flour, pork and potatoes. There were no luxuries except a gallon can, which was used indifferently for spring water, berries and to keep small game from flies,

---

[22] As those noises described in the 1869 novel, "Lorna Doone: A Romance of Exmoor," by Richard Doddridge Blackmore.

and two grape baskets, which are convenient for such small stores as tea, salt and pepper.

When we set out the wind was east and the sky but half clear. Loons were flying. We made our way to the head of the lake and found the carry without difficulty by steering just to the left of the last island. With this direction in mind the carry is not hard to find, for it is a winter road leading straight down to the lake across the bog.

VII — GASSOBEEIS CARRY

"We camped here but had hard work to find a place large enough for two men to sleep on which was not either full of rocks or covered with mud and water.

Our water to drink and cook with had to be dipped a few spoonfuls at a time from holes in the path and was the color of brandy."

Manly Hardy,
on Mud Pond Carry, 1858.

FROM Gassobeeis to Fourth Lake is not only a hard road but a long carry, not less than two miles — two good Maine miles at that, says Father, who has lugged on it these many times. We have several kinds of miles here— the short mile, the mile, the long mile, and "the good long Maine mile," which is the Scotch mile and a bittock.[23]

There is a story, now water-logged and condemned but still afloat, of the notoriously profane man who was so taken aback on discovering that

---

[23] Eckstorm makes more than a few references to Scottish sayings and literature. In the poem by Scot Robert Louis Stevenson, "A Mile An' a Bittock," the first line reads, "A mile an' a bittock, a mile or twa." A bittock, is a little bit, a short distance. A Scotch mile was 5,952 English feet, compared to the statute mile of 5,280 feet. Others may damn a carry as being measured in Irish miles, which was marked out as 6,720 feet.

the tailboard of his cart was out and his load of ashes was distributed the whole length of the hill, that all he could say was, "Swearing won't do it justice." More might be said of Gassobeeis Carry — nothing more apposite. I have seen all sorts, but though there may be worse carries, I have yet to see that kind. It isn't as blind to follow as some, nor as rocky as some, nor as long as others, and possibly not quite as wet; but in its palmiest days its water privileges very nearly equal those of the famous Mud Pond Carry,[24] and in its variety, which age does not wither nor custom stale, it completely distances that much condemned place.

Yet, in the encouraging guidebook phrase, "Even ladies have been known to undertake it." But an unincumbered man or even a woman ought not to complain of anything short of impassability. The tune changes when a man must stagger along over rocks, roots and swamps beneath all the load he can rise under, or still worse with a canoe on his head, than which no Eastern despot was ever more prompt to make one's neck the price of a misstep.

At the beginning of the carry the load was bound up into packs and lugging bands adjusted. I had secured two coats and buckled them to my bag — which by a long and persistent course of obstinacy I have secured the right to carry myself — and had just tied a pair of shoes beneath, when the fraud was discovered and the shoes seized as contraband. However, being rear guard, it was possible to secure something else, the can and a hatchet perhaps, after the advance was already on the march.

Off we started one foot before the other, at a pace very like a trot for one no taller than myself, Father at the head of the train, Jot next under a hump like a camel's, my mackintosh and rubber boots in the rear. We plowed through lambkill and rhodora waist high and wetter than

---

[24] The Mud Pond Carry is the most famous in Maine. For additional notes, see, "Hubbard's Guide to Moosehead Lake and Northern Maine - Annotated Edition." by Hubbard and Carbone, (2020). Burnt Jacket Publishing.

ordinary water. Slowly we waddled over a footing of sphagnum so thick and yielding that it was like walking on a feather bed laid on springs. There was a quarter of a mile of that soft footing on the carry, and, in spite of predilections for bogs already expressed, I think there are better places for carries.

Uphill we posted as if on the king's business, over stones and fallen trees, nor stopped until we reached the height of land. Our progress was made in fairly long stages, made as quickly as possible, with only short stops, following Father's rule for carries; *rest in walking back for the next load.*

"What will you have for refreshments?" I asked, as they went back for their second turn.

"Ice cream," said Father.

In their absence I provided them the best substitute which the woods afford — a heaped handful of snowberries (*Chiogenes hispidula*).[25] The tiny vines were matted over the old crumbling logs and all bore pearly berries. I had never before seen it fruiting so abundantly. This is the nonesuch of our berries, a little too good and rare for common use, but unequalled when enjoyed separately, when the gust is allowed to linger on the palate until the full savor of its spiciness is dissolved. It is the crowning achievement of the heaths — the most feminine of them all, pure in blossom and fruit as the snow from which it gets its name, delicate in all its structure, shy in its habit, and although hardy and evergreen wherever it is, reaching its full perfection only when it finds root and support, yea, and its life in that on which it lavishes all its graces and beauties and excellencies.

The second stage was short, extending only to the fork in the road where the index on the dead pine points to the left and the Machias

---

[25] Synonym for the *Gaultheria hispidula*. Native Americans had many uses for the fruit and the shrub from a sedative, to a beverage.

Lakes. On the left before you reach this is a "bear-biting tree," a pine, I believe, which Father pointed out to me. I should not have noticed it myself; and, indeed, it was not until I had seen half a dozen such, that I was able to distinguish them from trees which had been shot at, scored with a pick-hand spike or otherwise accidentally injured. The marks, which are from 8 to 9 feet from the ground, are often over grown and pitchy, and would not be taken by anyone but an expert for the work of an animal. They are found in firs, pines and spruces, most frequently in the former, and invariably, Father says, in trees that have a conspicuous place along some road or carry, at the fork of logging roads or the edge of a landing — never in the deep woods. The marks are made by the great canine teeth which are set in so deeply that they rend the tree as if a rifle ball had been shot through the side. Usually the same tree will be bitten many times by bears of different sizes or else several trees not very far apart will be marked.

"Tell the man who made that," said the old Greek painter, pointing from his friend's drawing to his own more perfect one, "that the man who made this would like to see him."

Because these trees stand in prominent places and the bears always rise to their full height in biting them, it has been supposed that they indicated, like the old Greek's line, the identity of the author. The tree on this carry has proved the correctness of the supposition. Several years ago when carrying across to Machias, Father examined the tree carefully. Returning a few days later, he was surprised to see a new bite so far above all the others that its height astonished him. Closer investigation of a mossy log at the foot of the tree revealed the tracks of a very large bear, who, shrewder than the rest, had stood on the log while making his mark. It was a plain challenge to the world of bears to bring forward someone taller than that. I wonder whether he ever saw it afterward and remembered his own cunning with an inward chuckle, for no doubt they do remember.

The third stage was long, very long it seemed, extending even to the crossroad to Unknown[26] and the Hemenway farm. It is this that gives the carry its bad name — rocky, mossy, slippery, the holes between the rocks filled with moss and water. Then there are slippery skids in the way just frequently enough always to catch you unawares, fallen trees here and there, and a good bit of swamp embellished with sawgrass, tall brakes, moss, rotting and slimy skids, hussocks which promise good footing till you land on them and water which may be mid-leg deep and may be a good deal deeper.

By the time the swamp is reached, the lugging bands have slackened and the pack has begun to sag. If you could, you would raise your hands to relieve your throat of the band which is choking you, but both are full. On every cramped and aching finger hangs a separate article which cannot be set down, and on you go splashing doggedly through the water or jumping from hussock to hussock, while the pack sinks lower and bounces harder and chokes more with every jump.

The mosquitoes which sit on the alders here from March to December rub their bills on their sleeves and pitch into you, seeing that you can't help yourself. A mosquito has no regard for the rules of the game. It may be your luck when you cross this carry in the dry season of 1891 to be able to call it pleasure. I admit that I could smile at it while experiencing it in a wet 1890, but not even my wildest dreams of pleasure include Gassobeeis Carry until it has been averaged in with so much else that the proportion of Gassobeeis is infinitely small.

We took dinner at the cross-roads — less dinner than table decorations, for while the men had been lugging their second turn, the woods around had paid tribute to me. Although it was well along in

---

[26] The chain of lakes known as Upper, Middle, and Lower Unknown.

September the ivory-leaf plums (*Gaultheria procumbens*)[27] of the year before were still hanging beneath their glossy leaves.

The fourth stage was short; memorable only because the cold which had been following all the way across the carry now overtook me and proved a misfit several sizes too large. It was the old story of taking too good care of one's self. To avoid getting wet I had worn my mackintosh and this was the result: The long skirt clinging to the wet rubber boots at every step doubled the exertions of walking, the rain on the bushes wet it from the bottom nearly to the waist on the inside and the perspiration condensing on the shoulders wet it from the top downward nearly as far. It was, in fact, a dripping rubber sheet. Constant exercise while waiting and careful wiping did not avert the mischief. Henceforward I eschew rubber garments unless it is actually pouring. Better by far to be wet and stay wet, cold and miserable, than be forced to cool off too suddenly. It is a poor constitution that can't stand considerable of the former, and the strongest should not be expected to undergo the latter.

The Machias end of the carry is even less cheering than the Gassobeeis terminus. The journal calls it "an unwholesome-looking place." In my own mind it is associated with the Ancient Mariner and "a million million slimy things." When you get here you will wish you hadn't come.

Marshes half a mile wide extend back to the "dry kyle,"[28] which fences the woods with dead trees, standing or fallen, grim, gaunt and gray. Loose-strife tangles the wet marsh and lily-pad and "moose-ear" half cover the stagnant stream which twists about without rule or direction, too lifeless to run straight. The place is given over to pickerel,

---

[27] Gaultheria procumbens is the name for the eastern teaberry, the checkerberry, the boxberry, or the American wintergreen. It is an understory plant in the blueberry family.

[28] Often noted as "dry-ki."

mud turtles and "slimy things that crawl with legs." Penobscot people call it Penobscot Brook, but Machias folk seem to know it best by the name of Cy's Gulch, an appropriately outlandish name, for gulch is a term seldom heard here and this is anything but a gulch.

Loon Shaking Off
(Editor's Collection)

VIII — POVERTY, KINDLING WOOD AND PHILOSOPHY

"He who is not contented with what he has,
would not be contented with what he would like to have."
attributed to Socrates.

PENOBSCOT BROOK enters Fourth Lake a little to the left of its head, Fifth Lake Stream a little to the right. The two would meet almost mouth to mouth were it not for an island of a few acres which stands between them. The island itself would have been a point still further separating the streams, had not the land behind sunk in times past, so that now there is only a wilderness of moose-ear above water. In former times this island had been Father's favorite camp-ground, and he did not like to pass without seeing it again.

He and Sebattis had camped there. He and John Spearen also. There Sebattis had lost his necklace of turtle's claws, and there Lonz as he stood on the shore fishing would swing his pickerel almost into the frying pan or make them run up the beach their whole length after the bait.

We turned out of our course to view the place, but Jot and I having no personal associations to be revived remained in the canoe, occasionally swinging the bow toward the rush bed in front and thinking what an altogether dismal place is Fourth Lake. A hurricane of last year had uprooted the pines along the shore of the island forming a barricade of brush.

On his return, Father reported that the cleared space behind was much more extended than formerly and the facilities for camping correspondingly less. Still the old spot looked so familiar and inviting that, although it was not yet 2 o'clock and the lake was calm, he decided to camp.

The fact is that five years before he had hidden here some favorite kindling wood, fat pine the like of which never had been seen in all the country, so black without, so yellow within, so pitch-imbrued that even the heat of the sun drew from it great resinous drops. He had always wanted to go back just to burn that wood. With such an attraction there was nothing to do but to camp. And yet it is my strong impression that before work was begun Father disappeared among the fallen pine brush and drew forth a piece of the shell of an old pine, five feet long perhaps and an inch or two thick. The wood was black and mossy and as heavy as if it had lain at the bottom of the lake for the last century. He was proud of it, but a more unprepossessing piece of timber never was seen.

If we camped on account of so small a matter as kindling wood facilities, the decision never was regretted. Four days and a half we stayed there in rain and wind, and yet the elements did not touch us nor the supply of "creatures with bones" fail us.

Thus, speaks the journal:

Friday —Rained. Lazy. Ate pickerel. Duck stew for dinner. Killed spiders. Had a cold caught on the carry.

Saturday — When it rains one can eat and sleep, but there is no time to write journal. It rained a downpour all night and blew like a piper. Father went out in it to see that the canoe was tied so that she could not blow away. It leaked a little through the tent, but none ran under us. My cold took most of my attention. We washed a little, read a little, fed a little and fished pickerel — until the pole broke.

Sunday — Clear and beautiful; even after two days' confinement we enjoy staying.

<u>Monday</u> — Still rains. * * * As provisions are likely to run low before we get back, Father and Jot went over to Shaw's on Dobsy[29] to get potatoes, sugar, salt, flour, etc. I stayed at home mending. When they came back they brought two wood ducks which Father had shot. Stayed in the tent all the P. M. and fought flies.

<u>Tuesday</u> — Still foul weather, but we shall wear it out yet.

But we enjoyed our camp here, although every rainy day shortened our vacation and put our desired end further out of reach, diminished our scanty store of provisions and increased the probability that the hidden stores at Nicatowis and Gassobeeis were spoiling. But present ease counts for considerable; with good wood to burn, a tent sheltered from the winds, a soil so porous that no amount of rain could saturate it and a never-failing supply of fish just off the landing, there was nothing desperate in the situation. Like our kindling wood, it looked a good deal worse on the outside than it really was.

If we had a good time here it was not on account of the weather, as has been shown, and certainly not because of any luxuries at our disposal except leisure; three people are seldom incumbered with so little of this world's goods when they can have all they want. Our pillows were our spare boots and rubber coats, our candlestick an empty cartridge. We had nothing to sit on except the bag of potatoes and a box which we had found. We had neither cards nor games, and our whole library consisted

---

[29] Hardy naming of Dobsy is referring to what is now labeled, Sysladobsis Lake, which is also known as Dobsis Lake. Shaw's was a supply depot. In years prior, bark steamers would operate on the locks between Dobsis and Pocumpus Lake. The name Shaw was common, but Thackster Shaw was a Boston-based tanner who operated a large tannery on Grand Lake Stream.

of one Harper's Magazine,[30] "Emerson's Essays," and two very thin pamphlets by Thoreau and C. D. Warner. We lacked even our usual copy of the Maine game laws, which we carry because of the satisfaction it gives when we learn that we have done the right thing in the right time. Indeed, we had very little of anything except pickerel and kindling wood, and none the less we were happy.

There is, of course, no virtue in this self-denial, although it contains a grain of philosophy which may explain our contentment. The secret is that we had nothing to take care of. We had bought our leisure at the price of all our unnecessary possessions and we were satisfied with the bargain. Money is only a convenient fiction; the real purchase is always affected by a barter of time for something which we fancy that we want more. Would you have a new hat or a new book? Then how much time will you give for it? Five dollars does not represent its cost to you, but the amount of time which you must take from your sleep or from your study to earn the five dollars does. Increasing our wants, our leisure diminishes; increasing our leisure, many wants must go unsatisfied. All this is very trite and world-old.

The Greek poet far back in the shades of antiquity sang,

"The gods sell all good things at price of toil."

In order to realize the truth in that statement, we usually have to get away from our neighbors. Living in a world where independence is less common than the boast of it, our ideas of what we cannot live without become super-saturated with our neighbor's opinions of what we must have in order to be respectable. We spend, dress, travel, not to please

---

[30] Mrs. Eckstorm was likely a lifelong reader of Harper's Magazine. In the appendix you will find that in the year 1931, a full forty years after this trip, she penned a letter to the editor about the name of Maine's Lobster Lake.

ourselves nor to give pleasure, but to purchase regard. We are the slaves of our possessions, nay the bond-servants of our conveniences also.

Even the labor-saving contrivance insinuates itself into our lives as cleverly as the camel of the fable pushed its way into the tent of its master. It has such good excuses for being there and it will give so much more exactness and leisure. Yet, it ends by making life mechanical and ten-fold more burdensome. Instead of handwork and free thoughts, we get the drive of the sewing machine. Instead of the easy-traveling quill, there is the increased correspondence and the galloping type writer. If bustle, hurry and push are the best of life, it is well to make getting the aim of it and use the latest machinery, but if our leisure seems delightful, why not, instead of submitting to the thraldom and slaving for these our servants, buy them off?

We can live without them if we only will think so. Go into the woods and let them follow if they dare! For all questions concerning the freedom and growth of the individual where can such satisfactory answers be found as in the woods? From this quiet hermitage the world has a very different aspect, as if we beheld it from the summit of a lofty mountain and saw it spread out below us, all its crooked ways made plain, its rough ones smooth and its jarring din subdued by the distance to a gentle humming. Here we can learn how a man's life is more than food or raiment and how it consisteth not in the abundance of the things which he posesseth.

Evidently many who go into the woods have not learned this. From the tin cans and empty bottles left behind it is plain to be seen that they could not feel themselves happy without everything that could be lugged, dragged or in any way conveyed up stream and across carries. The only limit to their wants is the inferiority of man flesh to horse flesh. Of course it is no more commendable for Socrates to be proud of the holes in his pockets than it is for Alcibiades[31] to be proud of his new coat.

> *He that hath not a kerosene lantern, ought not to despise him*
> *that hath one.*

But to insist on having all the accustomed comforts, to imagine that one's greatest pleasure lies in ingrafting upon the woods life a manner of living not adapted to the situation, shows how little sympathy for the woods is in the man, and foreshadows his almost certain disappointment. The possession or relinquishment of the things themselves is significant only as it reveals the man. He who will not trust the native balsam to give sleep and healing, clings to his inflatable rubber bed. He never learns anything about the woods, though he will talk most feelingly on the "hardships" of camping out.

The criminal lawyer, who is one degree more cautious, carries a straw bed with him, and this is his verdict:

> *"It may do for young folks but there is little pleasure in it. The*
> *anticipations exceed the realizations. The beds are not what they*
> *should be and the cooking is not always clean."*

But the two college students whom we knew only as "the plucky boys," who had crossed Moosehead and run down the whole West Branch — fair running, too; not wading — knowing nothing of canoeing, except what experience had taught them on the trip, though alone and with scarcely a handful of baggage apiece, and no food to speak of, said not a word about hardships and "outs," but insisted that they had a good time. This is a life of extreme individualism and self-dependence, and he

---

[31] It is thought that Socrates took Alcibiades (c. 450 – 404 BC) as a student to change his vain ways.

enjoys it most keenly who has most faith in his own resources and who depends upon himself rather than on the baggage which he carries.

On the one hand then, our contentment in the woods depends on our freedom to invent and imagine, and we declare with honest pride that no boughten article could be half so fine as our rather unsteady makeshift, which requires a little private propping; on the other, having few possessions, each acquires a higher value in our eyes. The empty box which we always expect to find near every camping place and which serves as a table, chair, and wash bench, is a finer acquisition than the most intricate folding camp-stool. The kindling wood which we had on the island was more satisfactory property than government securities. It had given us the pleasure of anticipation in the winter evenings at home when Father told us how he had hidden it against his ever going there again — he has many a cache of that kind or some other through the State, and many of them mouldered years ago, though he could still find the places. Then the pleasure of discovery, to find it still there after these years; of satisfaction because it was better than had been boasted; of pure aesthetic gratification because it had so much beauty locked up in it.

Whether, if we had gone in well supplied with patent kindlers, distrusting the existence of our own wood or our power of finding it, those four rainy days on the island would have been equally enjoyable, cannot be told. But it is not improbable that such faint heartedness would have destroyed our good hope and marked the time as a "hardship" of the sort at which guides curl the lip a little. Our wood, however, was something more than an old black slab which started the fire in the morning and hastened the cooking. It had in it a powerful genie — for genii are made from the fire element, you know — which came out whenever a bit of the wood was laid in the fireplace, and not only busied itself about the humble tasks which were expected of it, but quite transformed our meagre belongings with the graciousness of its company, cheered us by its geniality, took to philosophizing occasionally on its own account, and sometimes lectured on life, art, and ethics, to those of us who cared to listen. We burned it sparingly, not stingily, because we liked to see the genie, but as if its right to existence was as good as our own. We watched the dense, black smoke, the fierce, yellow flame and the pitch frying out of it. We watched it and spoke often of its beauty and good qualities, and no one ever hinted that the remark had not all the charm of novelty.

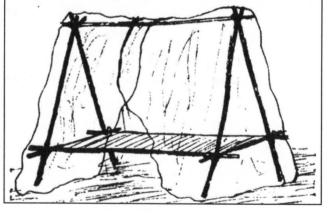

A HANDY CAMP BED.

CHICAGO.—*Editor Forest and Stream:* Some of your readers like to camp out, but do object to sleep on the ground. This is not the case with me, for I would rather sleep on the ground than in a feather bed. Still as all "outers" do not think or feel alike, I have put together a device that may be used as a bed.

A bit of canvas or duck of any required size, as say 3ft. by 6ft., is provided along the edge with eyelets, and to each eyelet is a short cord or rope. This forms the bottom of the bed; and it is to be used in this fashion in the woods. A few notched poles are cut and put together, as indicated in the sketch; and on the top of the four horizontal poles the bed bottom is put and the cords tied each to the opposite cord underneath the bed, passing the cord over the horizontal poles on the sides. This forms a can-

The Indispensable Camp Bed
An advertisement in Forest and Stream, 1891.

IX — ON THE MEAN ESTATE OF FOURTH LAKE

"Often four or five are seen in company, and I have known of seven. When swimming, one is usually in the lead and the others follow in his wake with short intervals between each, and when their backs roll out of water as they swim, three of four will often look like one body thirty of forty feet in length."[32]

Manly Hardy

FOURTH LAKE is about four miles long by a little less than half as broad, and as uninteresting as a butter statue. It has no features to speak of; three streams are connected with it, too sluggish to be called tributaries, and a horseback walls the eastern shore. Of sand is the shore, the steep bank is also of sand and of gravel brought here ages ago by the ice. About all the solid land to be found, the land which was always here, miles and miles of it, is largely under water. A few small islands in the lake on a foundation of solid ledge, by contrast with the main shore, strengthen the impression of mistaken economy and general ruin resulting, as if the bottom had dropped out of the region some ages since for lack of good underpinning. Fourth Lake is so unlike the rest of the world that it makes one feel as if he were hit with his own antipode and bound to stand on his head in order to keep up the illusion.

---

[32] On his death bed, Manly Hardy wrote his final essay, "The Otter," for Forest and Stream. It was sent by his daughter and published over several installments, beginning in the issue of March 4, 1911, Vol 76, No. 9, pg. 330.

Anyone who has lived on clean Penobscot waters, where there is good slate and granite under all, doesn't know what to do with such a Dutch country, and hasn't even a name by which to curse it. Bog it is not, nor swamp, nor marsh, nor meadow; nothing but literally "sunken land." We of the Penobscot have nothing, unless on the Mattawamkeag, which is not known to me, like this flat desolation of moose-ear, traversed by dead streams of labyrinthine crookedness and overhung of mornings with thick mists and the smell of rotting vegetation. The water is brandy-colored, full of suspended black particles, probably washed from the decaying moose-ear; not fit to use until it has been boiled.

The maps say that Fourth Lake lies north and south, with its outlet to the north; but I beg leave to differ. In September the sun doesn't rise in the north, and by the sun that lake lies about northwest and southeast, with the outlet in the latter direction. We didn't set a compass to determine it, but there are things which one knows without the help of the dictionary; and north is in every good woodsman's head so firmly fixed that he will believe his own instinct against map and compass, disregarding both if they don't agree with him.

"Map's wrong," he says, and off he goes following north in his head, as true as the wild goose.

He doesn't stop to look at the branches of the trees and the moss on the rocks and the other signs of the storybooks, he himself is a magnet. But it makes very little difference if the maps of this region are not correct as to direction, for there is no direction to anything here. Even the water doesn't know which way to run. You can paddle up Unknown Stream for the better part of two hours, facing every point on the card, and then not get where you can see out of the moose-ear, or put foot on dry land, or get to any place where, if the year is wet like this year, you can swim, wade or walk ashore.

Unknown is the third stream which connects with Fourth Lake, the largest, longest, dreariest of them all. It winds down from the Unknown Lakes, the crookedest stream in the world, unless perhaps Thoroughfare

Brook on the Allagash. After neglecting two or three gaps in the horseback by which the stream might have forced a passage to the lake, it enters on the left side about half-way down. It is a wilderness of moose-ear, a mile wide at least, fenced with dry kyle — that is, standing dead trees — and fish-hawks' nests. Sebattis used to call it "his farm," it is so flat and wide.

The moose-ear, by way of explanation, is the *Pontederia cordata*, better known elsewhere as "pickerel weed."[33] With us the *Brasenia peltata* and all the various kinds of *Potamogeton* are called "pickerel weed," so it seems best to retain the hunter's name of moose-ear, bestowed because the leaves resemble the long, narrow ears of the moose, both as more exact and more apt; for the *Pontederia* is not, commonly speaking, a weed.

Pontederia cordata – "moose-ear."
(Editor's Collection)

---

[33] Spelled both as, pickerel weed, or pickerelweed.

In single specimens the moose-ear is a beautiful plant, and as it grows on the margins of ponds in clumps of shining green, as clean and crisp as a calla, with spikes of purple loom dotted with gold, and played round by sportive insects. It is a pleasant, summery sight; but hundreds of acres of it, left on slimy flats by subsiding waters, or half submerged by the rising floods, browned at the tips and twisted by frost, looking (as Jot used to say) "as if it had been struck by the Spanish mildew," are enough to make one hate a place.

Fourth Lake is the rubbish dump of creation.[34] All the world stuff left over after the work was finished was dropped here — all the quag, deadwood, moose-ear, horsebacks and odds and ends not used in polishing that artistically uninhabitable country between Union River and the Machias; only here instead of bogs, barrens and boulders, we have the impassable sunken lands of Fifth Lake Stream, Penobscot Brook, the outlet, and chief of all— of Unknown.

There is a hungry, swallowing look about Fourth Lake. It is like some of the monsters of which we read it seems to be trying to cover its victims with slime, after which the swallowing may be taken as a matter of course. It is entirely in keeping that it should be the greatest rendezvous for sea serpents in the State.

According to the newspapers the sea serpent — he is always called the sea serpent, because he couldn't possibly be one — swarms about this lake. His chief business is to keep its waters boiling with his gyrations and to exhibit for the benefit of chance spectators. He is seldom less than 40, sometimes 80, feet long by the time the story gets to the

---

[34] Please, for those of you who love to fish and canoe Fourth Lake, when you leave a review for this book, consider these words were written by Fannie Eckstorm over 130 years ago. The reader will discover, her praise of Fourth Lake for the bounty they received, and its rightful place in the wilds of Maine.

Portland papers, and as he rolls out of water, he leaves a wake behind him proportionate in length to the credulity of the onlooker.[35] He has a way also of raising his head 3- or 4-feet above water, and no one ever fails to tell how it shines in the sun.

In one of the back numbers of *Forest and Stream* he crossed to a neighboring lake and carried off the body of a lumberman, breaking a 2-inch hawser.[36] At times he goes on shore and gorges himself on deer, and his track has been seen on the snow in winter when he came out to frolic on the land! The length of the tales and the veracity of the observer are always equal, according to the newspapers. Even though experienced hunters smile and say that the Fourth Lake sea serpent wears an otter skin and that his more common antics are precisely those of three or four otters playing together, the serpent has now been on duty for so long a time that he should be relieved and suffered to share the honorable retirement of the dingmaul, the side linger, and the walrus which used to frisk and gambol in the neighborhood of Chesuncook in the dimly historic period of thirty years ago.

A premium might safely be put on Fourth Lake as the most unattractive piece of scenery in the State, to which not even the efforts of the sea serpent have been sufficient to draw a crowd. Anyone not professedly a pot-hunter has no reason for going there. But that is just why we were there; our first and chiefest care was to get something to put in the kettle, and that can always be provided here.

---

[35] In the 1880s the Washington County lakes had their share of lake-monster sightings. As far away in Aledo, Illinois, the *Aledo Democrat* ran a story about the Machias Lakes Monster (Dec. 9, 1881). In March of 1882, the *Machias Union* ran a story titled, "Chain Lake Snake," about a serpent in Pocomoonshine Lake. I suspect these monsters had to locate to those chain of lakes, since to the southwest of Nicatous, Alligator Lake was already claimed.

[36] A thick rope for mooring or towing.

In the summer there must be many deer in the moose-ear land. In the old days, what a paradise for moose. The lake is full of eels, great ones, that come up to the water's edge during the night and carry off all the refuse they find, of white perch with usually blue throats, and of pickerel to tell of whose excellence would require a separate chapter.

We had expected to get all the ducks we wanted, but the water was so high that even a wood-duck could see all over the country, so that it was impossible to paddle up to them. And, besides, they are scarce, having been drawn north, we were told, by the wild rice planted on Mattagoodus and other Mattawamkeag waters. In the old days, in four successive mornings, Father once shot and saved twenty-eight ducks, which was all they could eat or give away; although Sebattis had a very pretty faculty for putting a great deal of good victual where "the bugs don't got him." A few still come late and go very early, and after sunset one may hear the good-natured wack, wack, wack, of the black ducks and the sharper week, wee-eek of the wood-ducks as they feed among the moose-ear.

(Editor's Collection)

X — THE FOURTH LAKE HORSEBACK

IF anything about Fourth Lake is worthy of special notice it is the "horseback," as kames, or the moraines left by glaciers are called from their shape.

Kames are so common here that we have ceased to regard them as curiosities, and wonder equally that strangers should see anything remarkable in them, and that they should fail to recognize as quickly as ourselves any trace of them. Kames usually show as rounded ridges, in appearance sometimes like an old railroad embankment, at other times a long, low hill, varying in height from a few feet to a hundred, of sand or loose gravel either clear or bearing pebbles and boulders, usually of granite and sometimes of great size. They cross the country every few miles, usually flowing south east, some barely traceable, some interrupted. Others like the *Whale's Back of Aurora*[37] continuous for miles, a conspicuous feature of the landscape. Some can be distinctly traced for more than a hundred miles, at their lower ends most spread out into kame-plains, of which the great blueberry plains of Cherryfield are an example.[38] The presence of ice-worn pebbles and disintegrated soil, usually sand or gravel, are enough to show even the tyro the road that

---

[37] Aurora, Maine, population of 114 (2010 census), is a town east of Orono, Maine and south of Nicatowis Lake. On Route 9 east of town, there is a turnout at which the Whale's Back could be viewed, but the trees on the far side of the road are so overgrown now, it is not worth a stop; videos, however can be found on the internet.

[38] Today known as the Blueberry Barrens, near Schoodic Lake.

the glacier used to travel; and on the tops of the mountains, northwest and southeast, almost as exact as the compass itself, are the scratches of the nails in the glacier's shoes.

The Fourth Lake horseback follows the left shore of the lake most of the way from one end to the other. At the upper end it crosses the lake — our island was a part of it — and reappearing, follows up the side of Fifth Lake Stream. At the lower end it turns at the carry to Dobsy Lake (for the very good reason that if it didn't turn there, the carry would have been somewhere else) and runs in a double ridge across to Dobsy. Thence it follows up the shore of the lake for half a mile to the end of Norway Point. Whether it still continues up the lake or across it to Pocumpcus and the Machias system of kames must be determined by those who know the country; as also whether the other end goes down past Fifth Lake to the Pleasant River system.[39] But its general course is of less interest than its action about Fourth Lake. Here it does something peculiar.

The Fourth Lake kame flows in a westerly or northwesterly direction for about three miles. Kames rarely take this course, and when they do so, unless compelled by some local cause, they flow from west to east. But this apparently flowed from east to west — for it is probable that it belongs to the Pleasant River system. What makes it vary from the normal direction? It would not be surprising if some things concerning the courses of glaciers yet remain to be explained, for wherever I have noticed the west and east horsebacks, as on the way from the West Branch to Katahdin about Middle Joe Mary Lake, there seems to have been no obstacle in the way sufficient to have forced them out of their natural south easterly course. And here at Fourth Lake there is no apparent cause for a deflection, much less for such an unusual westering.

---

[39] There are many online Maine Geological Survey Maps for exploring the horsebacks in this region.

If ever a glacier had an opportunity to run just where it wished to it ought to be in this flat country, with nothing to oppose or turn it aside. Exact observations may prove the real deviation to be less than I think; but the course of this horseback, if carefully studied, should throw some additional light on the causes of the direction of glacial movements.

The Fourth Lake horseback is from thirty to forty feet in mean height, composed of fine materials, sand, gravel and small stones. In places its whole side is laid open to the weather almost back to the line of its greatest height. At other points the side is just beginning to slip, and again the rounded top is entirely unbroken. Many kames are in worse condition, but I do not remember one which seems doomed to destruction in so short a time, from natural causes only. Father says that within the years he has been there his island has worn away perceptibly, although it is only a few feet above water.

How much faster will the rain and melting snow wash down the loose drift of the main kame, and the undermined trees tear away with them great masses of its substance. When once the kame is laid open to its main axis, the work will go on with quintupled rapidity. It is only a matter of time for this horseback to be reduced to a bar of pebbles and gravel. Then what? On a lake without a dam, it might not be so easy to predict; but where a dam alters the level of the water many feet during the year, so that at one season it washes the top of a bar and at another it mines its roots, changes go on much faster than under ordinary conditions. We can depend upon men to keep dams wherever there is a good water power or logs to be driven out.

To go back a little, the sunken land of this lake was undoubtedly caused by the flowage of the dam, which killed all the trees on what was once a flat cedar swamp, washed them away and planted moose-ear in their places. At whatever time the snow and rains shall succeed in carrying off all the fine materials of the horseback, the dam and the ice will combine to remove the gravel bar left behind. Then high water and ice together, in no long geologic future, but in time measured by centuries if not by scores of years, will scour out the sunken land of the unknown, behind what was once the horseback, until Fourth Lake will occupy a position nearly at right angles to its greatest length at the present day.

(Editor's Collection)

XI — FORWARD

Again the wild cow lily floats
Her golden-freighted, tented boats
In thy cool coves of softened gloom,
O'er shadowed by the whispering reed,
And purple plumes of pickerel weed,
And meadow sweet in tangled bloom.

from, *Birch Stream*
by Anna Boynton Averill

If it had not been that our ultimate point on the Machias, the old Hemenway Farm on Fletcher Brook, and the climb of Fletcher Mountain[40] for a view of Fifth Lake, required two consecutive days of fair weather, one for drying the bushes, the other for the trip, it would have taken worse weather than this to keep us four days on an island. But on Tuesday, although it was foggy and foul, we caught a few more pickerel, packed up our goods and started down the lake, determined either to run into better weather or to make it come after us.

The dam at the foot of Fourth Lake is not in good condition; and as some logs had been left side-boomed into the outlet there was a poor chance to unload our goods and take the canoe by. As we crossed the dam to look at it, a great blue heron that had seen the advantages for fishing afforded by a stream which had forced its way under the shore

---

[40] Fletcher Mountain is now, Fletcher Peak. Elevation about 838 feet.

end of the dam, rose within 10 feet of us. His neck was drawn back behind his shoulders, his head extended a little beyond the breast, wings only three-fourths unfolded and legs trailing, not dangling nor stretched out behind as in full flight, but held just as they had been when he had sprung upward — precisely the attitude in which the Japanese paint cranes rising to fly, a striking confirmation of the spirit and exactness of their pictures.

There is a carry of a quarter of a mile past the quick water below the dam, and we lugged one turn across. That one trip was enough. As the carry had not been much used of late, and bark-peelers had fallen hemlock logs across the path during the summer, Jot declared that rather than carry the second turn, "he guessed he would run it past."

This he did, and after affirmed that "the water was just nothing at all." It might not be well for the inexperienced water man to take Jot's word for this, though no one in camp ever doubted it even in the eleventh degree.

On the way across we came upon a flock of four partridges and shot all of them. Below the carry the stream is very pretty, resembling stretches of the East Branch Penobscot, notably that just above Stair Falls. Gnarled swamp maples, just turning red, and ash trees grew among the meadow grasses. By the water's edge grew *Osmunda regalis (var.) spectabilis*[41] with its masses of tropical foliage, and scarlet cardinals, as we call the red lobelia, reduplicating its redness in our speech just as in nature it is always doubled by its own reflection in the stream.

There were bits of meadow, some current and rocks in places. At the head of an island was a gravel bed, which we had to walk past, and not far below we heard the noise of a smart little fall, which Jot ran. Then we came into the flowage of Third Lake, like that about Fourth Lake, a long stretch of moose-ear and dry kyle.

---

[41] A species of fern. This is an older classification name.

A mile or two down the lake we landed on a sandy beach on the right side where a sea-wall is forming, and had our usual feast of pickerel. Jot said that he was getting ashamed to look a pickerel in the face.

While eating, I noticed little maple seedlings were growing in the crevices of the drift-wood. A log-cock (*Ceophloeus pileatus*)[42] flew by cackling, the only one I remember hearing on the cruise.[43]

We had hoped that it would clear off by noon; instead, it began to rain and blow hard in our faces, smiting us with heavy gusts whenever we came out from the lee of a point or an island. But we put on our rubber clothes and called it the best weather we had seen, since it could not keep us back.

Third Lake, though seven miles long, is narrow and has islands in it, so that it is impossible to raise a dangerous sea, and the shore, being rocky, bold and good, without sunken rocks, is a safe one for canoeing. Granite predominates, but it alternates with trap, with such abrupt lines of demarcation that if I only knew something of geology, I think I might tell a pretty story about it. The islands in the lake are small and pretty. At one place they make narrows only about one-fourth the average width of the lake, undoubtedly a great crossing place for animals, especially for bears. On the right, the shore growth is cedar, signifying a swamp

---

[42] The pileated woodpecker.

[43] "*The Woodpeckers*," by Fannie Hardy Eckstorm was originally published in 1900, it is a book of over 100 pages with illustrations. An expert on birds, in 1901 Eckstorm published her much more comprehensive text, "*The Bird Book*," with almost 300 pages. Manly Hardy, who was a respected ornithologist, had an extensive collection of over 3,300 bird specimens in his collection, lacking only 20 species which had a full number as designated by the American Ornithological Union (A.O.U.), now the American Ornithological Society (AOS). Mrs. Eckstorm assisted her father with his collection and she was an expert taxidermist.

behind. The left has considerable birch growth, pretty beaches and the look of a shore that affords good camping places.

We held to the right, although it was the lee shore, because this is straight, while the left is broken by deep bays and pockets and a long arm at the lower end. Father had told us this at the start, advising us to face the wind rather than take the longer cruise under the lee of the other shore. He had been here once only, twenty-three years before, when he had come up the lake guided by another canoe and had returned by a different route; yet now, after all this lapse of years, retracing the course in reverse order, his memory did not fail even details.

The outlet is blind. Usually one sees a break in the woods, a bit of low shore, the gates of a dam, or some sign of river driving which serves as a guide. But here all these were lacking at the real outlet, and at its right is a logan which has every appearance of the natural exit from a lake. The real outlet lies under a point almost entirely concealed by a long spit of sand which runs out from the right shore almost across to the point, so that one is tempted to sheer away thinking that the shore is continuous. Originally a narrow stream must have flowed quietly out of the lake between wooded banks, but as there was no chance to shore a dam at the outlet, the dam was placed about half a mile down on the stream. Its flowage makes a large pool which the sand spit already mentioned divides from the lake.

It was still raining when we landed above the dam, raining so hard that the camp stuff and myself were temporarily deposited under a river-driver's shelter of hemlock bark, which we shared with a large spider until the tent was ready. I tried to keep the water off the guns and to observe the spider; but she curled up her legs and observed me, the usual way with wild creatures when one has time to watch them.

Our larder was well supplied this night — one duck, four partridges, and five good pickerel. Why then the temptation which came to Father when he took his gun and followed the road along the stream to look out about the country? In the yard of a lumber camp, feeding among the grass and sprouts, was a two-year-old deer.

He saw the deer first. As it was raining, the deer did not smell him, nor see him until they were not more than two rods apart; even then Father lay so low, hat off, only his rubber coat showing, that the deer showed no alarm but continued to pluck grass and chew it slowly with one end sticking out of the corner of his mouth. He gazed curiously over his shoulder at the unnatural object in the hollow. He went away unmolested.

Even when there is no novelty or excitement in shooting game most people would like to know whether the gun would go or miss fire, or, at least, what would happen if they pulled the trigger. It was not from respect for the law that this deer saved his life, nor from fear of the wardens, but because he was a pretty wild creature and there were those four partridges, the duck and the pickerel to be disposed of. When Father told the story he met with our approval, which is more than good deeds sometimes receive.

Buck In The Woods
(Editor's Collection)

XII — WHEN IT RAINS

Through the glory danced the shower
To the thrushes' ringing measure,
And the rainbow sprang in sight,
— One foot o'er the hidden treasure,
Deeply in the bright lake drowned,
Where the gold may yet be found.

from, *The Sunlit Shower*
by Anna Boynton Averill

THE journal says nothing about it but I have an impression that it rained overnight. One of Father's rubber boots had been carelessly left leaning against the tent and in the morning it was partly full of water, as Father discovered when he put it on. I know that it rained in the morning, for the journal mentions it casually.

Even in fair weather Third Lake Dam must be about as dull as a sanitarium, but in a rainstorm there is positively nothing for a woman to do unless the fire burns holes in the family clothing or the men wear out their stockings. The men tried fishing which amused them and did the fish no hurt; they caught but one in two days. They also hunted for cranberries, but the water had been kept on so late that the cranberries were just in bloom and they found but a pint.

In the afternoon Jot came up to the tent lugging a great mud-turtle which he had seen asleep in the sluice way, crawled up to and captured. *His Turtleship* was highly indignant; he pawed and kicked, and bit at everything that was held out toward him; nor was he any better pleased when he found himself tethered to a stake in the dooryard,[44] tied by the tail, as that part of his anatomy best suited for such a use. He tramped about his limited course with the vigor of a thoroughly enraged fat man, looking ridiculously like a small elephant as he lumbered along with a swinging but uncertain stride, lifting himself high on those club-footed legs that were as loosely enveloped in skin as the true elephant's. His shell was about twelve inches long, smoothly plated, of a greenish color, narrow beneath. Jot called him a "toad turtle."

Henceforward Old Turk, as we named him, was a fixture in the dooryard; that is, as nearly a fixture as anything can be that several times in the day pulls its tail out of the nooses, hitches, knots and combinations by which he is successively made fast, or failing in this, jerks up stake and all, and walks off with it. Turtles know just where to go in order to reach water, but Turk always marched off into the bushes and crouched there with his head up, ugly and belligerent, when one of us followed up the trail. If he had not had this disposition to stop and fight, we might never have seen him again after some of his nightly escapades; for in a stern chase it was not easy to overtake the old fellow. He was not a flyer, but he had a good, long stride, and attended strictly to the business of getting away until he reached the cover of the bushes. If anyone thinks that the hare of the fable had a long nap that day when the tortoise passed under the wire first, it shows that he doesn't understand the paces of a turtle that knows where he is going. As for our keeping Turk, it was positively necessary. Having refused to eat deer meat when we might have had it, we were going to eat mud turtle when we had nothing else.

---

[44] In Maine, the area outside and near the front door; as well it might refer to the area near the backdoor, or the side door, or near the garage door. This is the first time I've seen it referenced in relation to a "tent door." Thus, any door will do.

Thursday morning was misty, but I could get down to the shore to wash, which was an improvement on ablutions in the camp-kettle cover, that cover being pointed and unable to stand straight unless propped up by all the spare boots. But just after breakfast the rain remembered what was expected of it, and came down in torrents. In half an hour over an inch of water was caught in a straight-edged basin. We staked the tent, and streaked it to make the water run down the sides and still it leaked. Then streams began to run in under the sides of the tent and to make little lakes in the middle of the bed. The blankets were snatched up, table knives seized and the overflow soon reduced through a channel which was called Case-knife Sluice, which may be described as rising in a bed of fir boughs and flowing directly into a fire-place.

It rained all the rest of the day, the only variety being Old Turk's occasional escapes and recaptures and speculations as to what kind of a stew he would make. Six meals had made a decided hole in our four partridges, six pickerel and one duck, but the pickerel were of good size, and by making the birds into stews we had been well fed, and had supper and breakfast insured before Turk's life was endangered. A stew is a very economical form of living in the woods. It is really a meat chowder, into which goes all the spare victuals you have, to be cooked together in a very black kettle. The advantages are that everything tastes of the meat in it and there is only one cooking dish to wash. Stews are prime favorites with woodsmen, who sometimes call them by the lumbermen's name, *swagan*, and sometimes by the Indian term *cosombo*.

In the afternoon Father went downstream and reported a foot of water in the road where there had been none the day before. He thought that by wading to the hips one might get down as far as the logan on the stream. Altogether, our prospects of seeing Fletcher Brook and mountain were no brighter than the weather.

That night we heard a mill whistle clear and distinct, and knowing that it must be the tannery on Grand Lake Stream we set our watches at half-past five. A little later we heard a gun fired somewhere on the eastern arm of the lake. It seemed strange to hear these evidences of man's presence when all around everything looked so solitary and remote.

After the supper dishes were washed it was our habit to spread down the blankets, and reclining on them look at the fire and talk as the mood came upon us. We did not meddle with general themes, but many were the stories of deer, moose and caribou, of hunters and lumbermen, and of points of woodcraft which would have made Thoreau forget all his lofty philosophy in undisguised envy of the material that there went to waste. Father had his own store of good things, and Jot's experience had been wider and more varied than falls to the lot of many. Everything had an interest for him. He had noticed and remembered with the instinct of a born naturalist.

Jot told me that the gray land turtles eat strawberries: he had seen them in fields with their faces red with strawberry juice. When I asked what ate the turtles, he answered that he knew nothing that did except bears. He told how he had seen a small hawk take five young kingbirds from the nest at one swoop, two in each claw and one in her bill perhaps, he could not tell the arrangement, but he knew fact.

He also had an interesting story about the shelduck. It had never occurred to me that it was any harder for young sheldrake to get out of their lofty nest than for young robins, although I knew that the young ducks had no quills for a long time, I had always supposed that they tumbled out with the heedlessness of the robin. But Jot told me — he had seen it — that the mother duck got them upon her back and flew down with them, leaving a string of ducklings behind her as she touched the water and they slid off. From the first they could run and slapper on the water just like the old birds. When they were tired, they climbed upon their mothers back again.

Of course, someone will doubt this. Perhaps the books do not tell this — I have taken particular pains not to see what they do tell — but Jot said so, and if the books disagree, they, like the maps and the compass, are wrong. The ducks may do something else; it is certain that they do this also, for it is an impossibility to doubt the word of an intelligent hunter when you know anything about woods' matters yourself. To doubt it argues, yes and proves, your own ignorance. They have strange things to tell, and the beauty of it all is that they expect you will believe them and do not think it necessary to prop up their own statement with the affidavits of Dick and Harry.

I do not know whether hunters tell these things to everyone, or whether, like the Ancient Mariner, "the moment that his face I see I know the man that must hear me." Certainly the good hunter tells strange tales but as Robin Hood said of Little John, "I have ever found him a very truthful man."

He brought me the *Epiphegus virginiana*, which I never had seen, and told me that the root was good for canker.

These were our usual evenings, but at Third Lake Dam there was a change in the order. We could not see the fire for the wind blew so hard that we had to keep the front of the tent tied in. Forced to depend on a candle for our light and cheer, and to listen to the beat of the rain on the canvas, which soothed us to sleep all too readily, we substituted reading aloud for conversation. As a means of keeping awake I do not think it was a great success. My conscience is clear, for I was the reader; but my audience were apt to seem suspiciously quiet until the reading ceased, when they suddenly became very much interested in the subject, but not quite sure what it was. They are acquitted; however.

It was an odd sight. The tent was not pitched quite straight so that there was a gap between the ground and the foot of it, which had to be filled in with the baker, our box (which we had found, as usual) and other articles. One tiny candle tied to a stick stuck into the earth shone no brighter than a good deed in a naughty world, and flickered in the draught. The family were wrapped in the blankets. I reclined on one elbow and in the intervals of streaking the tent when it rained through read, in a voice yet husky with a cold, *"The Uncle of an Angel"*[45] and *"What Some People Call Pleasure."* Could the genial author of the latter paper have imagined circumstances better contrived to make us appreciate the point of his tale — three people rain-bound, with nothing to eat but two or three messes of flour, a few potatoes, a little stew for breakfast and an old turtle tethered in front of the fire ready to be "next" whenever the word should go forth, and no prospect of its ever clearing off? We called it pleasure, and the proof is that we never regretted not killing that deer and leaving half of it to spoil.

In the morning when we rose the sun rose also, a welcome sight. Old Turk had evidently lost his courage, for instead of his nightly escape he had buried himself in the earth with only the top of his shell out. When we roused him, he put up his head with a mild, patient air, as if resigned to his fate. I was impressed that it was the same look which a captive missionary would cast on his cannibal captors and (without any disrespect to that gentleman in comparing him to a mud turtle) for much the same reason — not from grace but because he couldn't help himself. It was Friday — nothing on hand but a little flour and the turtle to whom we had become somewhat attached. To go down stream would take two days of pleasant weather. Then came Sunday, we could not get back to Fourth Lake until Monday if we had all good weather. We turned Turk adrift, and such was the affection that he showed for us that he came directly ashore again; the second time he was thrown in, he went down stream, but our bows were turned in the opposite direction.

---

[45] "The Uncle of an Angel," was a fiction piece by Thomas Allibone Janvier. It appeared in the August 1880 issue of Harper's Magazine.

XIII — TO SHAW'S ON DOBSY

*"Anyone who could cook as good a dinner as we obtained
there, could not cook a poor one."*

F. H. E.

IT isn't pleasant to give up what one has started to do, but in the present case discretion was better than courage. We backed out gracefully.

We came up the same shore which we had followed in going down, and picked a few cranberries that, oddly enough, were growing among the rocks on the beach. But most of them were still in bloom or just withered. As we approached the inlet we saw a canoe there, and going up found two young Indians fishing for pickerel. At first they were reticent, but they soon told us that they had come from Grand Lake by way of Wabash into the eastern arm of Third Lake. The gun which we heard the night before was theirs.

Just below the quick water on the inlet Jot saw the head of a fine buck which was standing in the bushes; but we made no effort to kill him. True, it was not a very good chance, but even if he had been standing broadside to us in the open meadows it might have been just the same, much as we wanted meat; for Father has been so much with the Indians that he is learned in their philosophy and never lugs an extra pound on a carry. Had he met a nine-prong buck on the Machias end of the Gassobeeis Carry, it would have been quite characteristic for him to request the buck to step across to the Gassobeeis end, because he always preferred to shoot his deer at Gassobeeis and save lugging them across the carry.

We thought it easier to carry past the little fall just above, many hands making light work, than to make Jot pole the load up over; for it is a "smart little pitch" and there was much more water than when we came down. At the gravel above we also walked by, and on the carry to Fourth Lake Dam we walked while Jot poled the canoe up. Third Lake rose fully twelve inches between Tuesday night and Friday morning. Fourth Lake had risen even more, though the gates were up at both dams. While we were at Fourth Lake the water rose fully two feet.

Such a beautiful, clear, hot day, such fresh air, such delight in seeing the sun after so many days of gloom. Even Fourth Lake looked almost pretty.

We left our canoe at the end of the carry to Lower Dobsy and went across to Shaw's to dinner, but more especially to get some flour, salt, sugar, potatoes, butter, condensed milk and matches, of all which we stood in some need, though we had plenty spoiling at Gassobeeis. The carry is a wide sled road, along the top of the horseback, a mile and a quarter from lake to lake.

Shaw's house lies about half a mile further up the lake on the end of Norway Point. Here the family receives summer visitors and cares for them at the house or on camping excursions to the different lakes about the region. The house itself is a commodious, two-story building, remarkably well located in every respect. It is in a grove of sapling red pine (which we call Norway pines), close to the lake, a perfectly healthful spot, free from mosquitoes, and though both cool and shady neither damp nor exposed to cold winds.

Mrs. Shaw is a lady of refinement and tact, with the art of making temporary visitors, like ourselves, feel at home. The board is excellent, for anyone who could cook as good a dinner as we obtained there could not cook a poor one. I have never seen a place in Maine to which it would be so easy and so pleasant to transport a whole family, old and young, and yet have all contented. Here old people could sit in quiet on the piazza, or children be left to play among the pines or to bathe at the beach in front of the house; while a part of the family could go off with guides and tents to hunt and fish. Twice a week the steamer comes up from Princeton, so that mails are regular and the place is easy of access.

We wanted to get some butter but Mrs. Shaw had none. Now butter is a luxury and according to our *credo* should be dispensed with. But as we made no pretensions to strict consistency in leading our life of poverty and self-denial, we have butter when we can get it. It was proposed that we should cross the lake to Ball's and get some. We borrowed a canoe and, forgetting that the absence of any baggage should make a difference in the way we loaded, got in after our usual order, Jot in the stern, Father bowman, myself in the second band. This brought her down by the head. The affair was managed with a real "Kennebec swing," as Penobscot people say of anything that is particularly awkward. Then the canoe herself was small, narrow and cranky, with a twisted nose, which, combined with the wrong adjustment of the weight, made her work directly up into the wind. There was no butter to be had at Ball's so that we had four miles of paddling for nothing. However, we saw the steamboat locks and ran across the narrow neck of land which separates Dobsy from Pocumpcus[46] for view of the latter lake.

Dobsy is not the proper name for this lake, but Sisladobsis.[47] I have used the common form of "Lower Dobsy" that I might distinguish it from "Upper Dobsy,"[48] of whose Indian name I am not sure. There seems to be an uncertainty about these names which is hard for a stranger to untangle. I have heard Sisladobsis, Sissisladobsis, Sissisladobsissis, and Sississis-ladobsissis given as examples of the perfection to which the Indians reduced their use of diminutives, each added sis being one more diminutive. But this looks to me more like an example of Yankee ingenuity than anything else. There seems to be something theoretical

---

[46] Pocumpcus is now spelled, Pocumcus.

[47] Sisladobsis is Sysladobsis on Maine Gazetteer map 35.

[48] Upper Dobsy is Upper Sysladobsis Lake on Maine Gazetteer map 34.

about it. In actual practice when anything is so much belittled as that last name, it would become a mathematical point and cease to have any visible existence; and so, I have thought of some of these lakes. But I do not claim to know anything about the matter, for these are St. Croix waters.

Lower Dobsy is a beautiful lake. When we returned to Fourth Lake we could not help contrasting it unfavorably with the clean shores, the pellucid water, the high hills and heavy growth about Dobsy.

As to our transport, we would not have exchanged our canoe for theirs. Indeed, they make a much poorer canoe there than we do on the Penobscot. We had with us our old favorite Lady Emma — named for the mother[49] — built for us by Gerrish, of Bangor, after a model specially shaped to meet Father's approval. She is a canvas canoe 19 feet long, made to carry three of us and all our load, yet light enough for one man to lug on a carry. She is high and full at the bows so as to mount a heavy sea, and yet narrow enough to be an easy canoe to pole up rapids. She has been used for three years now, all over the northern part of the State in the roughest water that we have. No one has ever criticised the model, some have copied it; but we who have been with her through hard places and heavy seas best know her virtues. She is as staunch as on the day she was built, and will see more service yet.

We paddled up the lake in the path of the setting sun and that night camped again on our island.

---

[49] Emmeline Wheeler Hardy, wife of Manly.

XIV — SATURDAY AND PICKEREL

"For a single meal the trout, but for a steady diet, broiled pickerel."   F. H. E.

FRIDAY night was as clear as a bell, with the stars out and northern lights flashing. In the morning we were teased by a bright sunrise, that led to mist, fog, and rain. Surely all signs fail!

We were back again on our old campground and at our old work of eating pickerel. Jot repeated his remark about being ashamed to look a pickerel in the face, and forthwith caught enough to last over Sunday.

Fourth Lake is full of pickerel. How many might be caught there in a day we do not know, for we never caught more than enough to meet our actual needs. In the present state of the game laws, when each one must be a law unto himself, we make our limit not one of times and seasons, but of the amount of game which we take, which never is more than enough to satisfy our appetite. Of course this is killing to eat, and according to sporting papers, not sportsmanlike; it lays us open to the reproaches of the elect, and classes us among those who have no appreciation of the proper methods for satisfying their thirst for blood. Nonetheless, we never kill when there is no reason for it; and like many other Maine people who have lost all respect for our game laws, we kill whenever we need meat. There is a volume yet to be written about Maine game matters, but it will be very different reading from what has been written up to this date, and it will explain things about which previously we have held our peace.[50]

---

[50] Eckstorm authored a series of articles for *Forest and Stream* (1891) covering Maine Game Laws from multiple sides of the issue.

The Fourth Lake pickerel were darker than our pickerel usually are, some of the smallest being very dusky on the belly and almost black above. Their average length was not less than 18 inches; and some of the largest measured 22 and 23 inches. I was always called a "biological fiend" and am still given to aruspicy,[51] so the pickerel had to furnish material for the note book. One female which we caught had a well-developed roe, although I had always supposed they did not spawn before February; and her head, after it was cut off and thrown into the water, continued to breathe with regularity and several times turned itself from one side to the other. Many undoubtedly have noticed the little sacs which cling to the gills of pickerel and also the great size and leaden blue color of the gall-bladder, and also how the long leaves of hard white fat cling to their intestines as to an animal's. I know no other fish in which the fat takes this form and looks so much like lard; a very good oil can be expressed from it.

It seems to be the fashion to slur the pickerel. But do not some throw more than their quota of stones? That he is an interloper in trout waters is true, but he is not morally responsible for his present surroundings. The same well-meaning unwisdom which supplied us the English sparrow and the black bass gave us the altogether more welcome pickerel. He is well-liked in this State. There is no other fish or game which the law allows us to take any time of the year, and the back settlers and farmers count on him as a staple article of diet, while to many who live in cities winter fishing for pickerel affords more sport — if sport is the criterion by which everything must be judged — than all the other fishing they get throughout the year.

---

[51] Aruspicy: a variant spelling of haruspex. In ancient Roman times this referred to someone who practiced a form of divination, by examining the entrails of animals.

The pickerel swarms when once introduced, he does not sulk like the trout, he can be taken at any time, and, practically, in any manner. Then, too, the pickerel is no mean food fish when properly cooked; but he will not bear being soaked in fat and taken out half raw, nor is he at his best in a chowder. Slit the fish down his back, cut out the backbone, salt well or corn overnight, then broil before an open fire and butter heavily. So cooked, they are the rival of the trout. For a single meal the trout, but for a steady diet, broiled pickerel.

It has been a matter of ceremony to praise and flatter the trout; there are those who cannot speak of them without dragging in the well-worn adulation of "speckled beauties." Indeed, they are a glorious fish but the pickerel has merits too, like Dr. Johnson,[52] despite his looks.

The trout is more fickle and dainty, the pickerel never lacks an appetite; the trout is shy, the pickerel bold to the point of rashness; the trout is playful, the pickerel is an old war dog. He is full of energy, dash, decision. When the buel[53] is rippling quietly through the water as if it were the only living thing astir, the ferocity with which some large pickerel charges after it and leaps upon it with a great whirl and a flash of black and yellow, never fails to startle. Then how he cuts and shears and hangs back, making the reel ring as he rushes for the nearest stick or lily pads, where he hopes to tear out the hook.

A trout does not know half as well what to do at first, but the pickerel never loses his head. A bold freebooter, a good fighter, a "leglar ole pilate"[54] as Sebattis used to call him, he has qualities which we Maine folk understand better than the trout's coyness. He commands our respect for his hardihood, independence, and unconquerable temper.

---

[52] Samuel Johnson (1709-1784), was a significant literary figure whose appearance was scared from, then, unknown health complications.

[53] See inset on Julio T. Buel.

[54] A saying of Big Sebattis Mitchell, "A regular old pirate."

There is a shark in him — see the teeth;
and a leopard in him — see the spots;
and a lion for courage, and a unicorn for strength.
One has but to look into the eye — what an eye!
What colors! what craft, what resolve, hate, rebellion,
tenacity of purpose gleam from the jeweled orb as he is drawn
up, captured, but not conquered!
Nothing but the toad has such an eye.

And for intelligence —
he has an unfortunate countenance, to be sure,
which does not give him an intellectual appearance, but his
cranium lacks none of the necessary bones, and he knows, just
as well as any other fish,
what he wants.

Annotated Edition

Julio T. Buel

In 1843 Julio T. Buel was eating his lunch at Lake Bomoseen in Vermont. His spoon slipped from his hand and descending into the depths, he saw a large fish grab at the twirling shiny spoon. In a moment of ingenuity, so the legend says he quickly procured another spoon from the kitchen, sawed off the handle, drilled a hole for the line, and connected a hook.

With his new invention, he was quickly catching trout that previously were elusive to his pole. Soon he was making the lures for others. With a patent on the Buel Spoon Spinner he became a fishing legend. The lure is still sold today.

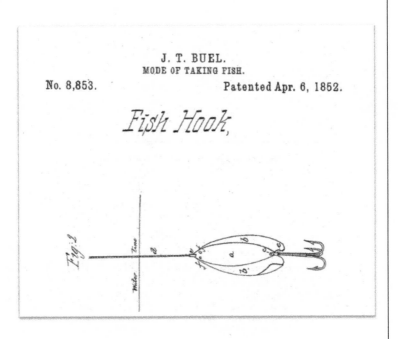

Image from U.S. Patent 8,853, "Mode of Taking Fish."
Inventor: J.T. Buel.

Advertisement For Abbey & Imbrie's Tackle

XV — SUNDAY AND SPIDERS

Of course Sunday was fair, and for that we were glad, since our Sundays in camp are occupied with the great enjoyment of whatever is nearest us. This day the sky was beautifully blue, and the lake, scarcely rippled by the light north wind, was blue also. I took my shawl and my Emerson out upon the knoll back of the tent and lay down there in the hot afternoon sun among the brakes, not to read, but to listen to the hum which underlies all silence and to enjoy to the full the sense of well-being which such a day imparts.

One might fall asleep on that hillock on such a day; perhaps one did. At first there was a procession of ants across one corner of the shawl, all stepping with sober haste, but unloaded and apparently going nowhere at all, unless to see the sluggard who had been directed to go to them. Then a dragonfly, with a red body, lighted on a brake nearby and solemnly nibbed his nose with his paw. I never yet saw a dragonfly do anything worth mentioning, except to whizz about like a portable windmill or to sit on a stick and duck his head and rub it just like a fat bald-headed man. Then there were strange voices on the beach — somebody must have been asleep to let Father and Jot pass so near unchallenged — and the visitors had to be reconnoitred through the pine-brush.

The tent was hot that afternoon, although I went there and turned the leaves of the Emerson, trying to read. It has been done so many times before, that sunshiny Sunday afternoons in the woods are always associated with Emerson. I do not care for him on a rainy day, when looking up to see if Nature herself does not smile approvingly on his optimism, there is nothing to be seen but a Scotch mist that dampened all one's ardor. "Heroism" and "self-reliance" need a background of blue sky in order to be perfectly picturesque, and the "compensations" of such weather as we had been enjoying for a fortnight are apt to look more like the retributions for folly than the rewards of wisdom. Not that Emerson is a mere fair-weather prophet; but, like all true poets, he has more of June in him than of November.

The tent was hot, as I have said, and full of flies; and a myriad of spiders, infinitesimally small, dangled from fine threads all over the roof. Big dragonflies three inches long, yellow or green, and black, bumped against the tent with a crackle of stiff wings and sat there as shadows. A red-bellied nuthatch lighted on the tent pole and looked in, then flew away. Emerson ceased to entertain. Then like Abraham of old we sat in the tent door in the heat of the day and looked abroad. The big dragonflies and their smaller cousins in red and brown were darting through and about the branches of a dead pine which stood in the dooryard about five rods off. We were watching their quick, whizzing, undeviating flight, in zigzag lines turned with sharp angles as they spun back and forth — are they not the pickerel of the air, motionless when they are still, swift as light when they move, arrow-like in the straightness of their flight, keen-sighted, voracious? — when we saw a spider come sailing over the treetops.

It was about three in the afternoon and the sun was at our left shoulder as we sat in the doorway. The spider came with the light breeze, which must have been drawing across the lake from the north, with a whole reef of web above her, which shone in the sun like a silver mainsail. As she came near a green pine tree she drew in her sail, clambering about on the rope ladders like any sailor, and descended to the pine of which she laid hold. When, after some hard work, everything had been made taut and belayed, she cast off again, this time sailing to the dead pine which stood in the clearing, a few rods from the green tree. The web did not catch; but she gathered it in and held it in her arms until she settled where she wished to be.

She made her way from branch to branch apparently carrying the collapsed web with her, very busy and agile, until she was on the side of the tree furthest from the wind, when once more she made ready her airy craft, spread her sails again and launched forth, sailing toward the sun beyond the reach of my vision and as far as Jot, who is an old bee hunter, could follow her course. What conscious pride such a creature, even though small, must feel in its ability to make, man and navigate its own craft on these long voyages across unknown seas.

I thought I had seen something when I saw this. I thought possibly it was something new and worth telling. But it was as much a pleasure as a surprise to learn by chance that the same had been observed and written down nearly two hundred years before by a lad of eleven. In the *Andover Review* for January, 1890,[55] you will find an article on *"The Flying Spider,"* written by Jonathan Edwards,[56] the great metaphysician and divine, when he was not more than twelve years old. If he stole my observations by being born a hundred or two years before I was, I will

---

[55] The quoted section is from, "The Andover Review – A Religious and Theological Monthly," Vol. XIII. January, 1890. No. LXXIII. Mr. Egbert C. Smyth (no title noted), reviews the writing of, "The Flying Spider : By Jonathan Edwards," written in an early letter when Edwards was eleven or twelve years old, approximated as the year 1714.

[56] Jonathan Edwards (1703 – 1758). Before his role as an American revivalist preacher, philosopher, and Congregationalist Protestant theologian, Edwards studied the experiments of Isaac Newton and wrote about natural philosophy subjects, spiders, and optics.

retaliate by quoting some of his. He has seen ten times as much as I, and has told it a great deal better, but he cannot capitalize and I will expose him:

> "I know I have several times seen a very Calm and serene Day at that time of year, standing behind some Opake body that shall Just hide the Disk of the sun and keep of his Dazling rays from my eye and looking close by the side of it, multitudes of little shining webbs and Glistening Strings of a Great Length and at such a height as that one would think they were tack'd to the Sky by one end were it not that they were moving and floating, and there Very Often appears at the end of these Webs a Spider floating and sailing in the air with them, which I have Plainly Discerned in those webs that were nearer to my eye and Once saw a very large spider to my surprise swimming in the air in this manner,"

This is only the beginning of young Jonathan's sentence; it is less than a quarter by actual measure. I pause to remark that ours was a very large spider, too.

> "they when they would Go from tree to tree or would sail in the air let themselves hang Down a little way by their webb and then put out a web at their tails which being so Exceeding rare when it first comes from the spider as to be lighter than the air so as of itself it will ascend into it (which I know by Experience) the moving air takes it by the End and by the spiders Permission Pulls it out of his tail to any length, * * * but if nothing is in the way of these webs to hinder their flying out at a sufficient Distance and they Don't catch by anything, there will be so much of it Drawn out into the air as by its ascending force there will be enough to Carry the spider with it,"

And so on for nearly a page more, telling us the philosophy of what he calls the "Greater Levity" of the web and the "Greater Gravity" of the spider.

He goes on:

"there remains only two Difficulties, * * * the One is how they first begin to spin out this so fine and even a thread of their bodies,"

Which he shows by experiments and drawings.

"the Other Difficulty is how when they Are Once Carried Up into the air how they Get Down again or whether they are necessitated to Continue till they are beat Down by some shower of Rain without any sustenance which is not probable nor Agreeable to Natural Providence. I answer there is a way Whereby they May Come Down again when they Please by only Gathering in their Webs into them again by Which way they may Come down Gradually and Gently, but whether that be their Way or no; I Can't say but without scruple that or a better, for we Alwaies[57] find things Done by nature as well or better than we can imagine beforehand."

He goes on discoursing on optics, astronomy and natural history, aged eleven they say, but the best mind in America even at that age.

---

[57] Alwaies, is the original spelling used in the Andover Review transcription of the writing, for Always.

And he has this corollary which has in it all the charm and restfulness of that lovely Sunday afternoon on Fourth Lake:

"We hence see the exuberant Goodness of the Creator

Who hath not only Provided for all the Necessities,

but also for the Pleasure and Recreation

of all sorts of Creatures

And even the insects

and those that are most Despicable."

(Editor's Collection)

XVI — THE RETURN TO NICATOWIS

The wind blew as 'twad blawn its last;
The rattling show'rs rose on the blast;
The speedy gleams the darkness swallow'd;
from, *Tam O'Shanter*
by Robert Burns

MONDAY again there was thick fog although we were up at sunrise, hoping to be off before the weather could remember what day of the week it was and make up its mind to rain. All our Sundays were pleasant, but on other days we had to take our chances.

When finally we did leave our island and head up Penobscot Brook it was with no little difficulty that we were able to keep the channel, for the water had risen until it stood within 2 or 3 inches of the tips of the moose-ear leaves and was so spread out among side channels and logans that it was almost impossible to follow the winding thoroughfare or to find the carry if we strayed from the stream.

The carry was exceedingly wet, so that, if the description of it had been left till our return, it must have received even a worse name than has been given it. Father engineered a side track past the wettest place, where, by the aid of the setting-pole and by stepping just as I was directed, I managed not to overtop my rubber boots; otherwise it might have been called wading, or it might have been called swimming.

The food question was as perplexing as ever. We had with us only part of a meal of broiled pickerel and we knew Gassobeeis would be too high for either trout fishing or duck shooting. But on the way across the carry Father came upon a flock of spruce partridges.[58] We do not count these as game, we do not usually even throw stones to scare them; for spruce partridges are commonly accounted as fit only for sable[59] bait, and never before had we been brought so low. Above all would we disapprove of shooting such a foolish bird with anything but a rifle, cutting its neck off in the good old-fashioned way. But in the present instance the rifle was far ahead, the shotgun handy and it was a question of dinner. Father ran back with the gun and soon, with more of the feeling commonly known as "resignation" than I had previously felt on the trip, I listened to the well-known bang, bang, bang of the old gun,

We were two hours and a half crossing the carry with only two loads apiece, and before we got over, the sun, which had been struggling with mists and clouds, came out. Gassobeeis was at least a foot higher than when we had left it. We followed the right shore closely, hoping to see a birch partridge[60] which we could exchange for one of our spruce grouse, until it became necessary to turn, in order to keep a straight course through the narrows toward the outlet.

The canoe had just been pointed out when Father and Jot, almost at the same instant, sighted a deer swimming quietly from the right to the left shore of the narrows. It was a lovely chase. The deer was on the base of a right triangle; we, with about four times as far to go, on the hypotenuse. If the deer was not alarmed, we could gain; if frightened at

---

[58] Eckstorm is referring here to the Spruce Grouse. Mainers had (and still do) call a grouse a partridge. Strict birders may not. The Ruffed Grouse (Partridge) is more common in Maine. The smaller size Spruce Grouse, which exist in far lower numbers in Maine, has no current open hunting season.

[59] Sable refers to a species of marten, not native to North America. As a fur trader, Manly Hardy may have referred to, and marketed, the marten as sable.

[60] The birch partridge is here referring to the ruffed grouse.

us, we must lose ground which we could never recover, for the deer would get ashore before we were within rifle shot. What little breeze there was drew toward us; on the other hand, we were heavily loaded.

The men sprang to their paddles without a word — no excitement, no haste, no great exertions; yet the canoe sped forward under the quick, clean strokes. The deer, too, swam well, but not very rapidly, and did not appear to see us, or seeing, not to notice us, until, when quite near the shore, yet too far off for a shot from a canoe. We saw the head turn toward us on the water and gaze curiously at us. The canoe was turned bows on, the paddling almost ceased.

The deer began to swim again more rapidly. It was not far to the shore now. On the moment up sprang the men, off came the coats, and then there was pulling indeed. This rush was the crisis. The water boiled behind the paddles, the canoe leaped with great bounds; loaded as she was, she flew through the water. The deer, too, was swimming fast, with a few strokes would have touched bottom, and then, with two bounds, a shake of a wet hide and a flirt of a white tail, would have cleared the bushes on the shore, safe from pursuit; but the onrush of the canoe was so sudden, the light shirt sleeves of the men and their unexpected rising so startling, the chase so hot, that the fugitive turned and began to swim away from the shore. The canoe shot inshore, lost headway, struck hard on a sunken rock. The deer was swimming with great leaps, shoulders out at every stroke — ten rods, eleven, twelve; it was the deer's turn now. The instant we struck Father sprang to his feet with his rifle. There were two sharp echoes from the hills, and our deer chase was over; but we were sorry that we had taken the poor, silly, useless, little lives of the spruce partridges.

That afternoon as we stayed at Gassobeeis, we could hear the wind howling above the trees, and we knew that there was a zephyr blowing on Nicatowis. It was better to be where we were. We picked some berries and after we hunted out our hidden stores. We were pleased to find them in very good condition— except our best hats, which, having been left in the dark so long, now appeared in a new light. Father's straw was decorated with a multitude of rosy spots, and my black felt adorned with a full coat of green mould. Father left his at Pistol Green later, but I had to wear mine down on the cars — it was that, or a faded red felt, or a Tam O'Shanter[61] that had seen so much of the world that the button was all worn off the top.

Toward night we heard again that mysterious sound, which rose from the earth and vanished — we knew not whence coming nor whither going; and again in the morning it went abroad. More than anything else I ever heard, it possessed me with a sense of indefiniteness and mystery. No animal crying in the night, no melancholy bird could have touched a chord that sympathized so nearly with that primitive feeling which gives rise to superstition; their voices might be unfamiliar or unrecognized, but there is not one among them, bird or beast, with which I am not intimately familiar, which I have not handled in the body or seen in life, and toward them I can bear no deeper feeling than curiosity.

None of the noises of the woods could have made the same impression; for I could account for them. It was none of the sounds made by men in their ordinary woods' vocations. Because it was unaccountable it gave an un-kin feeling, such as one might have toward a creature without a soul, for it seemed to dwell in a region apart by itself, away from the realities of the woods, unless the gnomes are real and make such noises in their burrowings. But what kept me from doubting my own senses was that we heard it with such regularity, morning, noon and at nightfall.

Our stay at Gassobeeis was entirely uneventful. We did not see even a duck. When we went down Gassobeeis Stream we noticed the change of color that had taken place. The bog showed more bronze than

---

[61] The wool Tam is a traditional Scottish bonnet. The name derived from the 1790 Robert Burns poem, Tam O'Shanter.

formerly. The withe-rod berries (*Viburnum dentatum*) hung in blue bunches, the wild raisins (*Viburnum nundum*) were a soft purple, the black alder berries glowed vermilion, and the scattering swamp maples were deeply dyed "all in a robe of darkest grain."

We ran all the dams and the quick water below the last without having to get out and without striking on the rocks, which much surprised Father, who had never seen so much water on Gassobeeis Stream. The stream is gradually growing up to weeds and bullrushes and needs to have another drive of logs rundown it to clear the channel, else in a few years canoeing on it will become very difficult.

When we reached Nicatowis there was a strong wind blowing. We worked along the left shore to Page's camp, took dinner there, and in the afternoon crossed the carry to the Upper Sabao, about thirty minutes' walk on a road that in ordinary years would be excellent and even in this was very good. So far as we could see it from the end of the carry, Sabao is a beautiful lake. Had the weather been better for the week or two past, we should have carried across and gone down this and the next two or three lakes.

When we got to Page's camp where we had left our canoe we thought it was blowing too hard to put out. So, not wishing to camp on the chips about an old lumber camp, we waited for the wind to subside; for we had seen in the morning, when we came out of the mouth of Gassobeeis Stream, an ideal campground — an opening on the left shore, under tall trees, on greensward as we thought, with a white beach in front, which our imaginations and the sunlight together made of sand. It was an altogether delightful spot.

Annotated Edition

"Lugging the Lady Emma - Sabao Carry."
Photo by Fannie Hardy.

The Lady Emma was a canvas canoe, which had started to increase in popularity in recent years, because they were light, dried out quicker than waterlogged birch, and didn't require to be re-pitched.
(Image courtesy of Special Collections, Raymond H. Fogler Library.)
The image may be mislabeled, or from a different trip, as they did not bring the canoe across Sabao Carry on this excursion.

We waited patiently for our opportunity. The wind lulled at last and we pushed off. A little way out and we wished we had not started. Westward everything grew black. Passadumkeag Mountain was shut off from view by an inky cloud, and the same black curtain overhung the sky. The lake was ebony and ivory under the shadow of the approaching squall, every wave-crest gleaming preternaturally white. If that squall struck us the Lady Emma would leave her bones on the rocks; or if we were borne back into Coombs Brook, there would be the rain. We pulled for the shore and our delightful campground. It was not far.

We reached the shore, tumbled our load out on the beach — it was gravel instead of sand — tossed it up over the bank, and in less time than it takes to tell it, had all our baggage snug and the tent laid over it, weighted down with heavy rocks. But think of our disappointment; instead of the beautiful grove we had seen under the morning sunlight, was an old hemlock-bark peeling and landing, cut up by roads, a side hill at that, so full of stones that it couldn't be much fuller. To make it worse, the tall trees, weakened by the removal of so many of their neighbors, often dead themselves, made refuge under them impossible. It began to patter great drops. For lack of any better shelter, we all sat down under the side of a bark pile to await the result with fortitude. We waited and it did not come; it even ceased to patter.

When we looked out, the squall was going round us. Well, we were there, and it was useless to pack up again on uncertainties. So we at last found a place where, by considerable digging, enough stones were removed to bring a little of the original ground to the surface. Father built a fire near the foot of a dead stump and I made great beds of hemlock boughs. Soon we had a camp good enough for our not over-tender consciences to praise considerably. It was snug and cosy among the hemlocks. We felt so rich with the addition of the rubber bag, provision box, and all the other articles which we had left at Gassobeeis during our stay at Machias, that we would not have envied a billionaire his gold shoes and gold umbrella.

Where else but in the woods can one so easily rise to, so long maintain, that high, heroic temper of Henry before Agincourt,[62] who in night and weakness and adverse circumstances "would not wish himself anywhere but where he was."

---

[62] Referring to Henry V, of Shakespeare's Henry V, who on the even of the Battle of Agincourt, urged his outnumbered men to recall the national pride in prior victories over the French.

Where else can one repeat with fuller meaning the prayer of Agur:[63]

"Remove me far from vanity and lies,

give me neither poverty nor riches,

feed me with food convenient for me."

Lake Rollers
(Editor's Collection)

---

[63] In reference to the prayer by Agur Ben Jakeh in Proverbs 30:8, "Give me neither poverty nor riches, but give me only my daily bread."

XVII — A NICATOWIS ZEPHYR

"The wind was blowing enough to bang the apostles."
Jot Eldredge

A loon cried in the night, not his halloo but his hoarse *haw, haw,* and we knew that we should have wind. We intended to get up early and be off before it rose: but when we turned out in the morning the wind had evidently been up all night. It calmed later and we hurried off. We did not stop to make haste slowly, but did the best we were able to reach the long point that forms part of the Nicatowis Upper Narrows. Half-way across and it sprang up again. It was not a tempestuous wind, it did not raise a sea, but it "pressed down upon the deep," as Virgil says, and when it was heaviest our two good paddlers had all they wanted to do to hold their own. But a wind never is continuous in its force, and in the lulls we gained.

I notice that poor paddlers pull a drawing stroke, reaching forward too far and bringing the work entirely on the muscles of the arms, straining the stomach if they work hard, which they seldom do. Those who sit in chairs do the same. But watch a man who is "strong on the paddle," and you will see that he does not reach very far forward nor exert himself until he has brought the blade back nearly opposite himself; then he throws himself upon it, pulls with the hand that is lowermost, and pushes with the other until the strong maple bends beneath him. He uses his whole body, and when paddling hard, springs from his knees.

To learn to paddle well one must either sit up on the thwart or paddle Indian fashion on one's knees, though few white men learn to do the latter. It costs too many hours of bitter pain of cramp and numbness. For the low canoe chairs so much in vogue I see no use. If the bowman wishes to paddle, shoot, or fish, he wants greater freedom of movement than can be had in a chair 6 inches high with a tall back to interfere with his elbows. And for a passenger's place in the second band there is nothing so luxurious as a seat made of the blankets folded flat and square inside the rubber sheets, with a cushioned back made by drawing down in front of the middle bar one end of the tent which is usually spread out over the load to protect it from water.

That was a day. By hard work we got in under the high sandbank on the upper side of the point, and drew up the canoe, waiting to see what the weather would be. At times it almost blew our hats off. When the sun was shining, we would talk of venturing out, and yet half a dozen times a scud of cloud was driven over us and it spit rain. We picked berries and waited, waited and picked berries, until finally, when it had become evident to our unwilling minds that no canoe could cross Nicatowis on that day, we reembarked and worked our way back to the Short Carry, keeping close under the shore to prevent being blown off.

The Short Carry is not a necessity, but a great convenience; it is, therefore, more welcome than the long carries which we cannot avoid when not inclined to burden bearing. It crosses the neck of the long point which forms part of Nicatowis Upper Narrows. This point is like the Irishman's barn, which was "a thousand feet long and one foot wide," and it swings out into the lake a full two miles, like a toll gate across the straight water route to Gassobeeis. Usually it is easier to paddle around the end of it than it is to carry the load across the narrow neck, with the extra trouble of unloading and reloading; but in windy weather the Short Carry, so called to distinguish it from the Long Carry past Nicatowis Falls, is a great convenience.

It was sunny and quite comfortable on the upper end of the carry — one might think the halcyon brooded there to make such a calm; and only forty rods away, at the other end, the wind was blowing and howling as if a legion of evil spirits were after it. Unfortunately, we could not camp on the comfortable end, it was so rocky; and Providence seemed to think us old enough sheep to take care of ourselves, for it made no effort to temper the wind at the other. But we were glad to be delivered from fear of falling trees; here were only second-growth birches and poplars which no tempest could uproot. Though we searched the woods for several rods on both sides of the carry, the only camping place we could get was a small spot in the middle of the carry near a poplar tree engraved with initials and the significant word "*Windbound*," showing that others also had been imprisoned here without being confined. Even this best place of all was so rocky that we could not pitch our tent with the usual upright fork for a front pole, instead of which we were obliged to use two forks braced against the ridge pole from either side.

It rained a few times while we were getting our tent pitched and our luggage under shelter, and then the draft across the carry caused an eddy round the corner of the tent and drew the smoke into our eyes so that it was unbearable; it was a poplar fire, too — add to previous notes that, for pungency, the smoke of a poplar fire, what little there is of it, will out rank everything else except the smoke of cedar bark.

We easily remedied this fault of the fire by making a wind screen of green trees which diverted the smoke. Father chinked the cracks under the canvas with boughs and Jot dug the superfluous stones out of our bed. I picked and laid a great bed of hemlock and cedar boughs, deep and fine, such a work of art that it consumed the better part of two hours in the making. For being permitted to make the beds in ordinary weather, the family sometimes enjoys sybaritic luxury in its cubicular arrangements.

It still blew, and the wind increased rather than abated. If the best canoeman in the country, in the best canoe, could have come across from Darling's shore to ours, it would have been as much by his good fortune as by his skill. We were snug and comfortable and, in the main, contented to be where we were. If anyone became a little restless in camp, he straightway regained his delight in the land by going to the end of the carry and looking out upon the angry lake, across which, as Jot said, the wind was, "blowing enough to bang the apostles."

Ducks In The Shallows
(Editor's Collection)

XVIII — DOWN NICATOWIS BRANCH

Rule for Carries:
Rest whilst walking back to gather the next load.
Manly Hardy

WE got off early the next morning while as yet the white frost made both ground and air chilly. As we approached Darling's, seeing no smoke nor any sign of life, we thought to pass unseen; but when we were still quite a distance away a man came to the doorway, and we caught the shine of a field glass leveled on us. We drew up alongside of the landing and the man came down for a chat. It was Charley Morey, of whose exploits I had heard so much — of his fleetness, strength, agility, and of his adventures with the sheriff, which have precisely the flavor of the tales of the merry green wood, and like them are not unpopular as a fireside entertainment.

Why should such stories delight us if they happened six hundred years or more ago in a foreign land, and yet their counterparts of today, or yesterday, happening close at home be passed by unnoticed? Here they are not so neglected. It is a fact worthy of comment, one without which the present attitude of the people of this State, toward the game laws cannot be fully explained, that many, if not most of us, were brought up on stories native to the soil, with our own Achilles the dauntless, and

Odysseus the crafty; or our own Wat Tylers[64] and Robin Hoods, who defied the sheriffs and loved the common people.

Each little place has its cycle, with its own list of heroes grouped about those of wider fame. What robustness and dignity, and, in time, what good literary form some of these acquire; the unimportant fades, the characteristic grows more clear, the figures rise into form and color and we have the beginning of an epic even in the nineteenth century. But to strangers these things do not appear so plainly, and they do not see the hold they have upon our imaginations; for we do not talk much of what most nearly affects us.

My childish Odyssey, preferred before the great original, was of tales of hunting on the Tobique with Leonard and Philbrook[65] and Peol Antoine Tomah;[66] and to this day my Robin Hood ballads read better with the names of living people. But it is a mistake to speak of Jock Darling as the modern Robin Hood; the situation may warrant a comparison, but there is no point of personal resemblance; Charles Morey, however, would make up admirably as Will Scarlet.

---

[64] Maybe a lesser-known figure, Walter "Wat" Tyler (?1341 – 1381), led, and was killed, during a peasant's tax revolt in England.

[65] Rufus Philbrook was a renowned trapper and friend of Manly Hardy. See inset.

[66] Eckstorm is referring to Hiram Leonard and Peol Antoine Tomah as the men Manly Hardy traveled with on a fur-hunt to New Brunswick around 1858. It is noted that Tomah's name has also been seen as, Pial A. Tomah. Examination of Manly Hardy's journals show his hunting on the Tobique in 1858 was with Leonard and Tomah; He did not meet Philbrook until 1859, and that fall the two partnered for trapping at Caucomgomoc Lake.

Annotated Edition

Rufus Philbrook

The hunting partnership between Manly Hardy and Rufus Philbrook began in 1859 when Manly was 27 years of age. Together they built a fourteen by ten-foot hunting cabin near Caucomgomoc Lake.

Mr. Hardy had this to say about Rufus Philbrook in the article he wrote about their time together.

"I found my partner a nice, clean fellow, never using either tobacco or liquor. His father had kept what was known as the Philbrook shanty, a stopping place for tote teams and lumbermen on the Nahmakanta supply road. His mother had been left a widow with three small boys and one girl. They were twelve miles from the nearest village with only one shanty between. Soon after her husband's death one of the boys died of the smallpox, and I have seen his little grave in the woods. This resolute woman did not give up, but hiring a man to do the out-of-door work, she for years kept the place, in summer scarcely ever seeing anyone, while in winter on some days she cooked for from ten to forty men a day. As the two boys grew larger, they helped as they could. Rufus began to hunt very early, as there was game close to the farm. As there was not a school within twelve miles the mother did the best she could to educate them at home. Rufus went one term to the Foxcroft Academy, paying his way by the skins and the bounty on bears he caught near home. A short time before we started, he had bought a place in the village of Brownville and had moved his mother and sister Sarah out among neighbors. Calling at the house in 1861, I saw the books Sarah had been studying and could see by the thumbmarks that she was well advanced in algebra and in Latin. Sometime in the 60's Rufus removed the family to Minnesota, and after hunting a couple of years, settled down to farming, while Sarah, after teaching in San Francisco, married a school teacher, and when I last heard of her was living in Arizona. The B. & A. railway now runs within a few miles of their old place in the woods, and the pond and the mountain west of it are now known as Philbrook's Pond and Mountain."

Manly's son, Walter Hardy, an artist, illustrated this article of his father, as stated in footnote 13, by Elizabeth Ring in "Fannie Hardy Eckstorm: Maine Woods Historian," *The New England Quarterly*, 1953. A biography of Walter Hardy is included at the beginning of the book.

The following images are from the original article by Manly Hardy, "A Fall Fur Hunt in Maine," *Forest and Stream*, Vol 74, 1910.

Half Pitch Camp
An illustration of the camp Manly Hardy built with Rufus Philbrook in the fall of 1859 when they hunted near Caucomgomoc Lake.

Stub Trap For Fisher

Father walked from the foot of the lake to the head of Nicatowis Carry, while Jot and I went down by stream. We found plenty of water. There were two or three sets of little rips, of which only the one just above the carry deserves a name. The rest of the stream is good plain canoeing. Nicatowis Falls, however, is called "very bad water." Although Morey told us that he usually ran it and others sometimes do the same. Watermen equally skilled, but less rashly adventurous, prefer to lug both their loads and their canoes two miles across the carry. Few who go to Nicatowis ever see the falls, for the road does not follow the river. But many doubtless have heard the story of how, one day in the spring when a heavy freshet was pouring over the falls and the drive had just got down to them, Isaiah Morey, father of Charles, stood up before all the men and gave them the dare, saying he would run that place if he could find a man for bowman.

No one could run it, that they all knew; but anyone around Nicatowis can tell you how Lon Spearen stepped out with, "I'm your man, Isaiah," and held him to it. They can tell you how Lonz followed the precept to obey orders if it breaks owners and held to his rope. With bowed heads, those there recall how Isaiah had nothing to say afterward except (with a sniff), "Didn't think 'twas so bad." When all the rest of the world has forgotten it, the owner of that batteau will still remember.

It was our own Big Sebattis Mitchell who ran Nesowaduchunk Falls on the West Branch one spring. Everybody knows what kind of water that is. Joe Aitteon — Thoreau's Joe — was at the end of the carry with the other boats' crews and saw him and his bowman make the leap. They had just lugged their boats across, but this was too much for them. They shouldered the boats again, staggered back under the load, put in and ran. Why tell of the boats crushed on the rocks, of the number drowned? The same thing happens too often. Joe Aitteon, at least, lived to be drowned at another place, in another way.

Only one more.

There are those four Penobscot Indians, well known to us, who in 1876 ran Canaan Falls on the Connecticut. The brother of one of them told the tale. It was unnavigable water, and they were in the eddy below the pier of the bridge which crosses the river just above the falls, holding on by a ringbolt waiting, when word went abroad that the Penobscot Indians were going to run the falls. People began to gather on the bridge. The Indians below looked up at the line of faces above them and below at the black water, swelling in ridges as it gathered its strength for its white plunge among the rock. Sappiel Orson was one, Sebat Clossian was one, little Sebat Solomon was one — better watermen never were: they consulted;[67] no man ever had run the place, man could not do it, but the honor of the tribe demanded it; it was a mistaken rumor that had

---

[67] In, "The Penobscot Man," (1904) Eckstorm relays, "There were four Indians in the boat, - Sebattis Solomon, Mitchell Soc Francis, Sappiel Orson, and Sebattis Clossian.

brought the spectators, but — the pity of it and the tragedy! — to disappoint them meant dishonor to the tribe.

"Old man, younk man, boy, gal, all sort, was there. Oldtown Injun she got great name ribber drivin'. We mus' go. We know it was die, but we mus'n' go back on our name," said the brother, speaking out his approbation of the act and his willingness to do the same.

They went. One died; three were saved by a miracle. They were drunk when they did it, they were unlettered Indians at best; but call up the knightliest knight of all antiquity, Bayard or Lancelot, and ask if he ever did a deed more noble, more devoted, more honorable to Honor, and when he answers Nay, I will call up four more like these, and four more, and four more, until he cries he never saw any army all so knightly. That is the Penobscot waterman. That is the kind of story on which Penobscot children are brought np.

At the upper end of Nicatowis carry, which is part of the woods road from Gilman's to Nicatowis, there is a hill and on the hill there is a camp, and at the camp we found a man who was waiting for Darling to come in from Lowell. Porter was his name, and for a reasonable sum we got him to answer to it and help us. But first we hunted around in the beeches and drew forth our hidden supplies, some of which were the worse for water, especially the potatoes and the angleworms. (Good gentlemen, we *do* fish with a worm when the fishes prefer worms). Frankly, the worms were all dead, having been drowned by the frequent rains.

This carry is the best two-mile carry I ever saw in the State, not excepting Northeast Carry. I claim to know because I lugged on it myself. Usually this is not permitted; and, being entirely under masculine control, and very submissive, I can seldom steal a chance to carry anything but my handbag. But in the present instance, as there was a little more than two loads for each of the three men, rather than have the expedition delayed while one man traveled two miles and back for a mere handful of small articles, I was allowed to be useful. True, I got Jack Mann's[68] load — two axes, a fish-pole, a frying-pan, a bundle of ropes, my heavy jacket and the two grape baskets— not much in pounds but a fine assortment for inconvenience. For the jacket had a satin lining and was as hard to hold as an otter, the frying-pan was not desirable as a near neighbor, and the axes and fishing pole utterly refused to fellowship; if one pointed east and west, the other two, pointed north and south, and to the zenith and nadir. But we all held together until we were across.

It is worth narrating that I inquired of our porter about that noise which we heard at Gassobeeis.

"Oh, you always hear that about Nicatowis," he replied.

I was piqued at the reply; it was just such an answer as woodsmen often make to greenhorns to put them off, and — is it going beyond the bounds of modesty? — there didn't seem to be any call for such an answer in the present instance. It was not so easy to believe in the supernatural when invited by another person; and so I told Father.

"It's the blasting on the foundations of the great pulp mills at Montague (Howland)," he said with an illumination, "thirty miles away, due west; that's why we heard it at noon and night."

But in justice to our porter, it should be stated that I am informed from a most trustworthy source that before a storm there is frequently heard at Nicatowis a rumbling like thunder, proceeding from the south, never explained, but conjectured to be blasting in the mines at Blue Hill.[69]

---

[68] Jack Mann is mentioned in, "The Penobscot Man." He was a woodsman who tended to many jobs.

[69] The Douglass Copper mine, in the Hancock town of Blue Hill was active from 1876 to the mid-1880s; with several trials into the 1900s, but only rarely being profitable during that time.

In the afternoon we ran down Nicatowis Branch to Pistol Green. For several miles the stream runs through meadows and rush grounds, with a strong current but no quick water. In places the rushes are, so thick that it is hard to free a passage. Further down, the right bank is low and wooded with swamp maple, while the left bank, toward which the stream sweeps and from which it retreats again with sinuous curves, is a high horseback, wooded with birch, maple, poplar and black growth. It is a part of that great Springfield-Deblois horseback which extends across the country for more than a hundred miles, perhaps the finest and most interesting horseback we have in the State.

Pistol Green, our camping ground for the night, is just above the mouth of Pistol Stream and a mile above the fork of the Passadumkeag, the most famous campground in the region from time immemorial.

XIX — UP MAIN STREAM

At noon the partridge beats tattoo;
At dead of night when winds are rough,
The loons sail up below the bluff,
And wake us with their wild halloo.
from, *Camp Solitude*
by Anna Boynton Averill

If it were not for telling those who have been there what they know already, the trip up Main Stream might just as well be left a blank; we saw nothing except people, did nothing except paddle against a strong current and there is nothing to tell except guidebook facts.

However, it is worth mentioning that when we reached the trout-hole which Al McLain spoiled by rolling in rock, Father heard a partridge drumming on the ridge back from the stream and started in after him. When he returned, he brought back the partridge, more pleased than if he had killed a deer. To locate a "drummer" by the sound, creep up to him on the log and kill him is the most difficult piece of hunting ever done in Maine. It requires the very best efforts of a born hunter, for the sound is very deceptive, it ceases the moment the pursuer gets in sight, they are many times shyer than a deer and, for some cause unexplained, shot seems to have less effect on them than at other times. Is it sportsmanlike to kill them so? Yes; and those who say it is not cannot perform the feat.

The Main Stream is principally meadow and crooks. A few rounded bushes, springing up among the grass do not relieve the monotony of the banks. Patches of pickerel-weed, moose-ear, and lily pads do not improve the paddling on the turns, which are so frequent that a long canoe like ours needs a hinge in her, as the hunters say, to work her round the curves. On the left, going up, Wyman Brook comes in. Cold Springs, on the right, is the first camp ground. We drew up here a moment to look at the signs, and Father announced that a large party had camped here not more than two nights before.

From the beds he could tell they were fishing, instead of hunting. Through the various signs he said they had at least two women with them; based on the new rubber tracks he investigated. He predicted that a little way up stream we should see a bright blue canoe, from paint he spied on a rock.

At Maple Growth, on the end of the carry to Spring Lake, we passed the blue canoe. At Lower Taylor Brook we passed two men, evidently of the same party, fishing. A little above we saw two women and seven men cranberrying – all as the signs had foretold.

Just above the bog where these last were, the stream grows narrower, with alders and wild raisins and, notably, the tall wild raisin (*Viburnum lentago*) which here reaches the diameter of six inches. The high bush cranberry (*Viburnum opulus*) is abundant also, though this was not a fruitful year for them. It is one of our best native fruits, the only sauce for venison when one has learned how to prepare it; but those who do not know how may be left to experiment for themselves, thereby increasing their enjoyment when they know how.

At this part of the stream, which is more tedious than any that precedes, is an artificial cut called the Lower Dugout; then on the right comes Upper Taylor Brook, where the trout are always dark-bellied, while those in the stream just outside have pink bellies. On the left above, is Brown Brook; then the Two Brothers, two good-sized rocks in the middle of the stream. Then comes more crooks, taller trees, and the Oxbow, where on the right, Dobsy Carry cuts off half a mile or less of stream. Further on is the Upper Dugout, and above, the ponds, in which the Passadumkeag takes its rise, and the Indian Carry to Upper Dobsy.[70]

The way was long but not tedious; every turn suggested some incident which might or did happen there and the succession of turns and stories rivalled in number and continuity the similar series of which the fair Scheherazade[71] made herself so agreeable. From his hunting trip here with Lon Spearen twelve years before, Jot detailed all the scenes in Lonz's adventures with the fire, and Father told with effect the story of the man at Cold Springs who mistook sandpeeps[72] for game, while Mr. Fairbank's public-spirited service in cutting off the big end of a green ash tree which had been felled across the stream while everybody else went around the top, was not forgotten. And like Dinarzade[73] in the story, we said of each one, "I find this the most entertaining of all: pray give us another."

Just below the carry to Upper Dobsy we shot a duck and heard a partridge drumming. To hear partridges drumming in the fall of the year bodes foul weather; but Father's treatment of all such bad signs reminds us of Tom Dana and the robin. This time, however, the partridge got away wing-broken, and probably hid in some of the rotten cedar stumps which abounded there. We trailed him five or six rods and lost the sign where the cedars were thickest.

---

[70] As noted earlier, also known as Sisladobsissis Lake.

[71] The legendary Persian queen who is the storyteller and narrator of *One Thousand and One Nights*, also known as, the *Arabian Nights*.

[72] Sandpeeps – a very small sandpiper.

[73] Dinarzade – a (mis)spelling of Dunyazad, the younger sister of Queen Scheherazade. In The Arabian Nights, to prevent Scheherazade from execution, Dunyazad tells stories with cliffhangers.

As this was only a short distance from the carry we decided to camp here for the night. Such a bed and such fire! Sancho Panza[74] blesses the man who invented sleep; but no man should stand higher in the calendar of Maine saints than he who first taught the virtues and the uses of good dry poplar.

Annotated Edition

The blessing from Sancho Panza is also given first billing in the poem by John Godfrey Saxe (1816 – 1887). Saxe was a Vermont born lawyer, satirist, and poet. The first two stanzas are quoted here.

Early Rising

"GOD bless the man who first invented sleep!"
So Sancho Panza said, and so say I:
And bless him, also, that he didn't keep
His great discovery to himself; nor try
To make it — as the lucky fellow might--
A close monopoly by patent-right!

Yes; bless the man who first invented sleep
(I really can't avoid the iteration);
But blast the man, with curses loud and deep,
Whate'er the rascal's name, or age, or station,
Who first invented, and went round advising,
That artificial cut-off, — Early Rising!

---

[74] Sancho Panza, the fictional character in the novel *Don Quixote* written by Spanish author Don Miguel de Cervantes Saavedra in 1605.

XX — THE CARRY TO UPPER DOBSY

"I don't believe there is another man in the United States that could have lived through what I have. I have been fairly chowdered all up."

Wild Bill Barrett

The next morning it rained. On Machias it had been necessary to wait for the weather: but here, as we were not intending to lug on the carry but only wished to see it and the lake, a little rain could not hinder us. So, putting off the execution of our threat against rubber coats and mackintoshes until we should get where we did not need them, we sallied forth to cross the carry. There was a slapping of wet rubber garments, the ghostly, empty sound of rubber boots walking and the soft *squush* of the same withdrawn from the suck of mud and moss. Three miles and twenty rods that carry measures, and all the way over and back there was the sound of the flapping and the walking, and most of the way it rained right merry marching music.

The carry to Upper Dobsy is a good one. There is a little low land near the Passadumkeag, which, on the present occasion, was wet; but most of the way lies across a rocky ridge, rising, heavily wooded and with much good hemlock still uncut, gradually from the stream. The road is easy to travel, but would not be easy for a stranger to follow because it has been so cross-hauled and blocked by trees felled into it. Apparently, it has been little used of late. If there has been much travel from Main Stream to St. Croix, it has probably gone by way of the old Indian Carry from Weir Pond to Upper Dobsy, since that is only a third the length of this.

As we went up the Passadumkeag slope, Father told us of a smuggler, who, years ago, had died on this carry when on the way across from the Provinces, and who was buried here. The spot had been marked by a fence of logs, rudely but substantially put up, as men mark Mortality, seeking to defy it. But Time had mossed the logs and gradually had mouldered them to the general level. When last he saw the place there had been nothing to mark it— a little hollow sunken like a cradle and a round-boled beech tree once blazed with some rude mark or symbol at the head. After the years that had passed since then, he was not sure that he could recognize the place. But he knew it by intuition, though now the lusty beech showed scarcely a mark on its round trunk, and the little hollow, which is yearly growing less, will soon reach the level of the surrounding earth. The smuggler's grave — we stood by it a moment in the mist, without gloom or disheartenment. Even there Life had conquered Death; in place of the signs which marked Mortality was the living, growing tokens of the Immortality which succeeds.

There are many such graves in the woods, "under the sod and the dew, waiting the Judgment Day." Murder and accident and disease each have their graves, equally unmarked and equally indistinguishable. They say that there are four on the old Indian Carry just above. Last year at the head of Pamedumcook the pseudo-guide, whom we dubbed the Professor of Woodcraft, told us a long story about a number between Pollywog Pond and Rainbow Lake; which may not be true, for the man is the champion liar of the State since Uncle Bill Barrett died.[75]

---

[75] See inset on, "Uncle" Bill Barrett.

Annotated Edition

"Uncle" Bill Barrett

On February 16, 1887, *The Boston Weekly Globe*, published an article, "CAMDEN'S VETERAN. Old Man Barrett Who Lives on the Turnpike." He was known as, Bill Barrett, the Camden Mountaineer, Wild Bill, and also, Crazy Bill Barrett.

He was a legendary Maine storyteller, fur-trapper, and hunted throughout the State of Maine and into Canada. Being the fur buyer he was, Manly Hardy likely crossed paths with Bill Barrett, either in the woods, or near Camden. For Camden is where the Hardys summered. According to Elizabeth Ring,[76] on the Hardy family times spent in coastal Camden, "there was hardly a road, beach, or back pasture, she later wrote, that she did not go over with her father. "Lilies in Rockport Lily Pond, I have picked them by the armful, and blueberries on all the hilltops that bore any and some that did not. Raspberries from the cut-over jungles and botanical specimens from everywhere." After years of tenting there during the summers, the family built a cottage on Dillingham Point where Fannie Hardy went in the summer until her marriage in 1893."

---

[76] In, "Fannie Hardy Eckstorm: Maine Woods Historian," The New England Quarterly, 1953. Elizabeth Ring was a correspondent of Fannie Eckstorm for several years. Ring (1902 – 1997) was born in Orono, and received her Master's Degree in History from the University of Maine (1926). She taught at high schools in Plymouth, NH (1923-25), Westerly, RI (1926-30), and also Maine history at the University of Maine (1938) and Bates College (1939-40). The article of note is a biographical sketch of Fannie Hardy Eckstorm.

The Hardy association with Camden, could certainly explain Mrs. Eckstorm's use of the term "Uncle" for Bill Barrett.

Barrett died November 11, 1889. Seeing he was written about in the Boston papers, his reputation for a storyteller preceding him, Mrs. Eckstorm could have been referencing this Bill Barrett of Camden.

If one were to search out all these tales of the woods there would be a strange collection of them. They range from the story of the retributive justice which faced Old Dirty Donald at his ending;[77] to that of Nolan's murder; from the grewsome tale of Larry Connor's skull;[78] and to the simple incident at which smiles and tears are blended, of how Joe Aitteon's boots hung for years in rain and shine at Shad Pond, where they found him, viewed with respect by all the river-drivers, a strange but touching memorial of their affection for the governor.[79]

---

[77] The 'ending' of Dirty Donald is told somewhat correctly in, "Hubbard's Guide to Moosehead Lake and Northern Maine – Annotated Edition," Hubbard and Carbone, 2020. See the section on the Musquacook Lakes. Full more on this story, as documented by Eckstorm, see, "Katahdin, Pamola, and Whiskey Jack. Stories and Legends from the Maine Woods," by Tommy Carbone.

[78] "The Grim Tale of Larry Connors," is told by Eckstorm in, "The Penobscot Man." Connors died busting a log jam. When they found his skull the following spring, three miles below the jam, it was placed in a fork of a tree for all to see, as a means for the lumbermen to pay their respects.

[79] Original footnote from Eckstorm: The antiquarian should be cautioned against mistaking for these relics a pair which I once left hanging upon a tree near the outlet of the same pond — much traveled shoes that had seen the whole of northern Maine, a good deal of the country between Glens Falls on the Hudson and the pinnacle of St. Armand, that had climbed Katahdin,

On the height of the ridge between the Passadumkeag and Dobsy, and about three-fourths of the way across (for the short, steep slope is toward Dobsy), is the old Dobsy farm. For many years cattle have been pastured here in summer and the old barn kept in repair; but when last seen the little shanty on the place was yielding to the assaults of time and the weather. Therefore, we were somewhat surprised to see that the little house had been patched up for habitation, and that an effort was being made to reclaim the farm from life-everlasting to live-for-ever.

They say that from this point, which is the height of land between Penobscot and St. Croix waters, there is a grand view of Katahdin; but it was lost on us. A thick mist covering everything, and the pouring rain, in which we made our appearance, must have made our little pleasure trip appear a highly quixotic proceeding to the three men in the barn, who suddenly were aware of a rubber-coated procession, armed with gun and hatchet, emerging from the mist close upon them.

We went down to the lake, but it was scarcely more visible than Katahdin. The water was very clear, and it must be a pretty lake, for there are hills about. A feature of the carry-end is a large scarlet-fruited thorn of unusual beauty, laden with fruit, the nearest to being edible of any thorn-plums I ever saw. This is damning with faint praise; but, from Father to the contrary, I am persuaded that the excellencies of the thorn-plum, as Thoreau admitted of its relative the wild apple, are not inherent, but depend on the forgiving disposition of the eater.

---

and woe's the day they ever were left behind, that should have been made to travel from Shad Pond to Mattawamkeag that hot August weather instead of the new pair that took their place.

A View Of Katahdin - *(Editor's Collection)*

We called at the little farmhouse on the way back, and, finding that the eldest of the men had known Rod Park,[80] with whom in his youth Father had hunted and fraternized, we spent some time there. To have known Rod Park is a passport to favor. A famous rifle shot and deer hunter, as well as a widely-known lumberman, popular even from the stories which such a reputation multiplies, Park had also that magnetic power which attracts and repels; he had enemies, but his friends he drew close to him, and those who knew him, such was his selective power, are no strangers to each other.

On the way back we noticed where a bear had been trapped in the summer — late in June or early in July we judged from the leaves on the dead alders — and from the fur around, it was evident that he had spoiled

---

[80] In the original writings, Eckstorm incorrectly noted the typing error of Park as Parh. She mentions in her errata, "I shall have more to tell about him later. — F. P. H." Those mentions were included in her series on Maine Game Laws. She said of him, "Park was a Veazie lumberman, well known all over the State, an admirable marksman both at game and target, a fine still-hunter for deer, an expert at all outdoor games and employments, the most buoyant, whole-hearted, irrepressible, fun-loving and laughter-making man that ever drew violin bow and loved his friend's quarrel better than his own."

while in the trap. He had been caught in the alders by the clog of the trap becoming entangled, and in his efforts to get free he had chewed and torn the bushes until they were beaten into brooms. There is, or was, at Pistol Green a hemlock tree which had the top, where it was fully six inches in diameter, gnawed entirely off by a bear that had climbed it with his trap and become caught up among the branches.

After dinner there was some delay on account of the weather and a discussion as to whether we should lie about the camp for the afternoon, or, taking our chances of rain or shine, go on downstream. Our temper is of the kind which grows more valiant when the odds are against us; and we started out. It must be twelve miles to the Fork and we were three hours making, for though the current was with us, the turns of the stream were so frequent that every few moments we would lose our headway.

As we got to the Fork and the early twilight began to draw on we discussed the chances that someone else would have taken our camping place at the Green, as well as the good pile of dry poplar which we had left against our return. Our uneasiness increased the nearer we got, until — as we poled up the swift Nicatowis Branch, now on one side of the stream, now on the other, wherever the bottom was best and the water shoalest, scaring our old heron from his perch among the maples — we became quite apprehensive. It was a relief to find our fears groundless.

Wood and camping place were both undisturbed. Of course our tent poles and pins were there and our wood ready; but though we camped from 40 to 50 yards from the stream, in seven minutes by the watch we had our tent pitched and our fire burning.

Settled For The Night

XXI — COOKING

THE next day we had duck stew for dinner; partridge also. I suppose even though small game was very scarce we got two of each on our way up and down Main Stream. But in these days the bill of fare was not of prime importance, and the journal ceases to mention it. Jot's best efforts were now expended in the preparation instead of in the provision of food.

There are people who do not consider cooking a profession, but Jot had a higher idea of it. He was master of half a dozen trades, but if he had a point of pride, I believe it was his cooking. He went about it most methodically. A given amount of hair combing and hand washing was the initial step; then the food was prepared with equal neatness and system: the kettles were put on, and the cooking proceeded to the accompaniment of some appropriate tune like, "O think of the home over there."[81] No interruptions or difficulties ever seemed to interfere, and fried, boiled, broiled or stewed, the food came to the table neither underdone nor overdone. I think it was science that accomplished this, for my own bumble endeavors were always unsuccessful and I laid the failure to lack of science; but Jot knew it all and could explain every wherefore. When I tried to make a dish of the cheerful beverage warranted to do no harm, it tasted of the tannery rather than of the tea caddy; they told me that it was smoked because I had not put the cover on the kettle. What town-born cook would ever think of her tea being

---

[81] A hymn by Rev. Dr. DeWitt Clinton Huntington (1830 – 1912).

smoked? I have done more things than that which are set down as sins against Hygeia[82] — let us not talk of them.

At home, economy consists in using every scrap of food and the least possible fuel. In the woods, it means the preparation of what you have in the least time and in the simplest manner. At the last reduction, one becomes a question of money and the other of dishes. In the woods we call dishes of all sorts "cooking tools." There is a homely candor about the phrase which I admire. It makes no attempt to raise these useful articles to the rank of ornaments and unessentials. It does not seek to disguise the fact that their utility is the sole excuse for their existence. It expresses in the most satisfactory way this principle of economy and selection. If any one word contains the whole sum and substance of true economy of time, labor and money, it is that word "tool."

Many years and more experiments have reduced our kit of "cooking tools" to such shape that it is neither heavy, bulky, nor inconvenient. Excepting two or three odd articles, the whole is packed in a heavy ten quart camp kettle with straight sides and a pointed cover — three large tin plates, two small ditto, two straight-sided tin basins of three and four quarts' capacity, two camp kettles holding corresponding amounts (one kettle iron, the other of tin for tea, both with covers and with ears riveted on to prevent melting), four tin dippers with handles nesting inside each other, three large spoons, three small ditto, three knives and forks, and besides these, when convenient, pepper and salt shakers and the dish cloths and wipers. It takes three days' practice to learn how to pack that pail. When this is done, the cover is tied on to prevent the loss of time or articles in case of a stumble or an accident. In camp the large pail is used for a water pail and the cover becomes a hand basin.

---

[82] Hygieia was the goddess, or the personification, of health, cleanliness and hygiene in Greek, and Roman, mythology.

A few articles are not included with the rest of the kit. The frying pan is always tied up in a piece of burlap kept for the purpose, so that it goes very well, only when swung on the end of the setting pole it acts like an insane pendulum — for, of course, it is a long-handled frying pan, as all which are used in the woods must be. In the old-time lumber camps, before stoves were used, 4 feet was the regulation length of the frying pan handle, and a boy was often employed to tend it. Far more useful than the frying pan is a little ten or fifteen-cent bread toaster, of the sort which fashion at one time allowed to appear on parlor tables as a photograph holder when decorously appareled in a bow of orange ribbon. It is perfectly flat, weighs but a few ounces, is easily cleaned, and is a great advance on the primitive sharpened stick for broiling fish, fowl, or venison. A folding baker is also a great convenience. Ours is made in exactly the shape of the old-fashioned baker which was formerly used in cooking before open fires. After the baking pan is removed it can be folded into a flat sheet of tin, the sides lapping in, the narrow back falling so that the long legs on its lower edge come flat against the lower reflecting tin, and the upper reflector dropping over all. The baker serves not only for bread but also for baking fish and meat. The reflection from the two sloping sides, above and beneath, upon the baking sheet cooks quickly and evenly, and when the surfaces have become dull a little scouring quickly restores the brightness and good cooking qualities.

With these simple "tools" Jot could prepare a dinner fit for a king, and never was monarch more liberal of his praises to his cooks than we to ours, as Jot himself will testify.

1884 Advertisement For Canned Soup

XXII — CLEAR WATER AND WOODS HOSPITALITY

"Good gentlemen, we do fish with a worm when the fishes prefer worms." F. H. E.

THE peculiar feature of Pistol Green is the soft green sward and white clover which cover it. Grass is a rarity in the woods; the weeds come early, almost before the lumberman, but only the lapse of many years and the frequent presence of man will make these civilized grasses grow in the wilderness. Pistol Green from time immemorial has been a favorite ground for camping, and this is attested by its deserving the name of Green, which, in our State, is very uncommon. Another sign was a part of the thigh bone of some large animal, which we dug up from several inches beneath our camp floor. Moose, ox, horse? — we asked which it was, and all judged it to be moose; for it had been cracked Indian-fashion to obtain the marrow. It is a long time since there were any moose in this region, except as infrequent stragglers.

From the Green several paths diverge; most are drivers' paths used only in the spring. The central one is the carry to Pistol Lake — two miles if we go all the way by land, but on high water like that of this year, it is not necessary to carry beyond the head of the roughest water.

I asked why Pistol Stream got its name, and was told that it was because "it went just as if it had been shot out of a little gun." An entire stranger would know it at once from this description. It is what woodsmen call "smart water" with a good strong "spring" in it.

Has it never Impressed anyone unused to our Maine woods and ways that we have a very peculiar feeling toward running water, calling it "good," "bad," "mean," "wicked looking" and so forth with a seriousness which so far exceeds any figurative or rhetorical intention that it seems to impute personality and moral responsibility to the element?[83] There is something Greek in this: so came the gods about.

Pistol is beautiful water, clear enough and beautiful enough to make dear old Garvin Douglass,[84] could he but have seen it, as I wish he might have, write an epilogue to every book in the Æneid in its especial praise, telling us more about:

> "The sylver scalyt fyshis on the greit
> Ourthwort cleir stremys sprvnkland for the heyt"

Abol has richer colors, more of the crystalline iridescence of the iceberg, as if it held an imprisoned rainbow, more of the translucent emeraldine tints of cold caverns brought with it from its birth out of the side of old Katahdin, more absolute purity; but Abol is not navigable. And Millinockett has the spring and the impetuosity, but without the same pellucidness. The charm of Pistol is that it is itself.

We poled up it in the clear, cool air of the morning, as much delighted as if it were a fresh creation made for us alone. The stream came down like a highway through the trees; ferns on the shores, waving half-vines, which we call "buck bean," in the water. The tall stalks of the cardinal flowers were now brown with ripeness that erewhile had lighted up the banks with their flames. Clean gravel in the shallows where the water was clearest, led to a rock-ribbed channel where it flowed faster. Great granite boulders lay along the stream, worn concavely to the height of several feet by logs and spring freshets. Rocks in the bed of the stream

---

[83] As opposed to water that is not 'running,' being labeled a "dead-water."

[84] While Eckstorm, or the typesetters of her work spelled this name, Garvin Douglass, it is meant to be Gavin Douglas (1474 – 1522). See the footnote in Chapter V. This passage, written in his Scots translation of the Æneid, has to do with silver fishes (maybe herring) lying on a bed of gravel near a stream.

made it give continual little hops and leaps to get over or around them, as it ran from one side to the other along its devious course, like a Naiad[85] pursued by the great god Pan.

The first Pistol is a beautiful, rounded lake, apparently about two miles long, with high wooded shores, partly pineland and partly hardwood, rising highest on the side toward Nicatowis. The edges, especially near the outlet, are set with great granites both above and beneath the water, which in a heavy sea would make canoeing difficult.

As we knew that Alonzo Spearen, of Passadumkeag (the Lonz so often referred to), and his partner, Sanford Hodgkins, of Burlington, had a camp here, we hunted it up. Lonz was not at home and his partner we did not known personally, but, in woods fashion, nothing would satisfy him unless we promised to come back to dinner. There is a heartiness and cordiality about such a welcome that entirely masters me. This man did not consider the difficulty of getting supplies in to the camp, hauling, boating, lugging and poling them so many miles, it did not matter that he did not know us, we were friends and welcome to half of the last biscuit if it came to that. And that is the kind of cordiality to be found everywhere through the woods unless it has been chilled by unresponsiveness of those who are ignorant of our native customs, have failed to return the welcome extended or, as some unfortunately have done, have taken unfair advantage of hospitalities offered them.

Less is expected of strangers now than formerly; but it used to be a common complaint among hunters, explorers and others that the elite of society who came here "hadn't no manners; they didn't know enough to invite a man to eat with them." As long ago as Thoreau's day, Joe Polis felt called on to reprove him for his discourtesy in not visiting old blind

---

[85] Naiads of Greek mythology are a type of female spirit, or nymph, presiding over fountains, wells, springs, streams, brooks and other bodies of fresh water.

Thurlotte in his hut on Mud Pond Carry, for this is the true significance of the incident which Thoreau himself relates. Much experience has caused the gradual remission of civilities to strangers unless by speech and action they prove themselves of native stock; but thirty years ago the same were extended to all, and no one asked the name of his guest unless he chose to give it.

After promising to return to dinner, we set out for Spring Lake, which lies between the inlet to Pistol and the Main Stream, outletting into the latter. It can be reached either by a short carry or a long one. We went by the latter, going up the sluggish inlet, where we saw signs of otter, until we got to the foot of the quick water, where a horseback comes down. The first part of the carry lies along this horseback through an open growth of Norway pines. We saw a number of bear-biting trees along this ridge and several bear traps adapted to all grades of ursine stupidity — none of Hodgkin's and Spearen's work, however, who know how to set a trap. The rest of the way is wet and boggy underfoot, though not an open bog.

Spring Lake is a jewel, the perfection of regular shape, clear water and shining white bottom. A little gem, with a cincture of prismatic colors, from the autumn-changed leaves upon the shore, playing about its margin in reflections of red, green and yellow, like the lambent flames of a noble opal. The shores are of broken granite, and the bottom being of the same, finely crushed, shows better than sand would the clearness and sparkle of the water, which welling up from springs beneath, fills this granite bowl with liquor brighter than any wine. It may not look on all days as it looked on this; but never on any day did I see so much beautiful water as here about Pistol. It was an experience not to be communicated by words.

There are large trout in Spring Lake. A man whom we met said he caught one the day before that measured 19 inches in length and 5 inches in depth. We were told that in Pistol they got white perch measuring 15 inches.

When we got back to the camp, Lonz had arrived with the gentlemen who were staying there. We were even more warmly welcomed than at first. Nothing was too good for us. The "wicket" was ours while we stayed, everybody in it was at our service. It was like having a crowd of powerful genii spring up at the rubbing of the ring or of the lamp to do our bidding.

They prepared us a dinner of the best the land afforded, fully equal to Jot's best efforts. They showed us the camp and offered us anything they had. We did want some salt and had brought a little box to get it in; but when we made known our want, our entertainers would not think of giving any one so little and packed up a large baking powder canister, as much as we should have used in a month, bidding us not to think of taking less, for salt was cheap — cheap after it had been brought all that distance! — and we had much ado to escape carrying off ten times what we wanted.

We were urged to stay overnight, pressed to remain, and our refusal was barely accepted; indeed, it was a temptation when we thought of the stories that would be told about the fire that evening— Jot with downright earnestness, Lonz with irresistible drollery, Hodgkins with quiet gravity equally entertaining, Father carrying a freelance on all topics, and the rest of us joining in or listening as the ball of conversation came to us or rebounded.

The camp is, as its constructors claim, "a snug little wicket" of logs, with a roof of split cedar, large enough for at least a dozen men and several ladies. It is in the midst of a fine hunting and fishing country, the best of scenery on all sides, and within easy reach of four lakes besides First Pistol. Built primarily for the use of sporting parties, it is resorted to by some who care only for the scenery and rest. Many ladies go there. The gentlemen whom we met at the place declared in their enthusiasm that the next year should see not only themselves but their wives there. We were told that next year the camp was to be improved by the addition of a separate cook room; though, if I were to be there, I would beg the privilege of sitting in the kitchen to look on, for both the partners are famous cooks, as well as first-class water men, workmen and hunters.

Somewhere on the trip Jot told us a story of Lonz which I had heard before from another source, of how, when a boy of sixteen working in a lumber camp on Birch Stream, he saw a moose track, and starting out with nothing but a three-dollar shotgun, a half-pint tin cup and a little uncooked oatmeal. The boy followed on the track for five days, sleeping in the snow without blankets and crossing both the Piscataquis and main Penobscot rivers, where they were open, on rude rafts, at last overtaking the moose in the town of Lee, where he killed him and sold him for a good price before returning.

In the afternoon we started out to see Side Lake, which lies to the right of the Pistol Inlet at the end of a two-mile carry, but we were not permitted to go before promising to return to camp again.

The carry to Side Lake, which is one of the Pistols, was partly bog, though most of the way good walking through tall growth, hemlock partly, I should say, with a vague remembrance of feathery saplings. Some of the undergrowth was beech. Near the end, the carry divides, one part going to the Third Pistol and the new right-hand branch to Side Lake. With the sun in the quarter where it now was, Side Lake was softer in its color than the glowing gem of the morning, but even clearer in its transparency. It was absolutely calm, and looking down we could see the bottom for a long distance from the shore.

A canoe and paddles lay nearby, but we would not ruffle its tranquility. To me, such clear, still water suggests solidity more strongly than anything else, so that the comparison to glass or marble seems not only highly expressive, but the only allusion properly explanatory. It is not the surface of the water alone, Milton's "clear hyaline, the glassy sea,"[86] but its depth and body, so to speak, which, in proportion to the

---

[86] From John Milton's poem, *Paradise Lost*, 1667.

transparency of the water, gives it more and more this appearance of being a solid block of glass, an underworld in which the fish are imprisoned. Our clearest ice looks scarcely more impenetrable than such pure still water to which may be given the fine Horatian phrase, *splendidior vitro*, not of surface only but of depth.

We tarried awhile, watching the little fishes, and tossing in bits of moss and dry twigs to see them rise and draw under the coveted but disappointing morsels. We wished we had something better to give them; but finding that they learned nothing from experience, gradually withdrew our repentance and kept up our sport. They were beautiful, both chubs and breams, though the latter had put off their brilliant summer garb of green and copper color and scarlet, and were now but shadows of their former splendor, recognizable only by the black spots on their gill covers and their pretty motion. A fish out of water is a coarse, clumsy, limbless creature; in its element it is sylph-like.

We stopped again at the camp, according to our promise, and again were entreated. The camp and all that was in it was ours to control, use, or carry away. But we had a tent standing with open doors on the Green, and we steered out into the blaze of the declining sun.

Father walked down the carry, not to overload the canoe, as the water seemed to be falling, and Jot and I went down by stream. A changing color hung in the treetops, amethyst or purple, or between the two. The first chill of early evening lay along the stream. From the shadows of the trees the great rocks stood out more boldly, and the little ones lifted up their heads where the waters parted round them to rejoin in a trailing ripple. Still others hid beneath the crowning current, which mounted them smoothly on one side to run away in white-curled wavelets on the other. There was no sound above the voice of the stream but the ring of the metal-shod pole on the rocks as, now dipped on one side now on the other, it directed or restrained our progress.

We went back across the lower part of the carry at the time when, earlier in the season, the hermit thrushes would have been at vespers; but it was too late in the year for their music. Instead of their melody there was stillness throughout the woods, until Jot, coming after with the canoe on his head, gave a cheery hail as he passed on down to the landing.

Poling A Canoe
(Image from, *Woods and Lakes of Maine*, by Lucius L. Hubbard)

XXIII — GRAND FALLS AND SPAWNOOK

We know by the leaves and the bending grasses
That the wind of the south goes by today,
A viewless spirit that softly passes
"Over the hills and far away."

from, *Over the Hills and Far Away*
by Anna Boynton Averill

WE went downstream in the chilly morning, saying good-bye to our old heron as he sat hunched up under the trees on the sunny left bank. Off behind a swamp we heard a partridge drumming, but not being anxious to wait in the cool, did not encourage Father's going after him. At Trout Brook Landing we were willing to go ashore and exercise to get warm.

It lacked an hour or two of noon when we reached the head of Grand Falls. These are a mile long, rough water all the way, ending in a natural fall, improved for driving purposes by a rolling dam about 14 feet high. That is my own version on my own judgment. Well's Water Power of Maine gives the falls as 200 rods, the total fall of 100 feet, the last pitch at 20 feet. I do not know about the length of the falls, but that carry is full 320 rods by my reckoning, and I carried on it a varied load from my slippery jacket and the rifle down to whatever could be clutched with the other hand. If any benevolent-minded person said that it was twice as long as Nicatowis Carry, I should try to believe him unless he could prove that the jacket was just twice as slippery as it had been there. I do not pretend to know the total descent of the falls, though it is considerable. But as to the last pitch I have an opinion, though rather than quarrel with Well's Water Power, I would compromise, stretching the height from 14 feet to 15 feet, if the opposing party will throw in the other 5. It is a good fall, though, and pours down a flood of white water.

Father and I each lugged a light load across, but Jot, after running ahead a little to look out the place, said "he guessed he could go it all right." It is bad water at any time; even in a dry season Big Sebattis declared that it was "berry rabbidge water" and took "great deal of judgment" to pole up it. But this year the stream was 2 or 3 feet higher than Father had ever seen it in the fall, and the increased volume of water pouring down over the falls made them much worse than usual. The rains had so swollen the river that it boiled down over the rocks in great white rapids that showed a brandy-colored edge above the yellow foam when the sun struck on them, rapid after rapid, increasing as they descended until, just before it made ready for the grand leap, it was all foam.

After waiting some time, part of the time on the bridge watching the water, and part of the time in the bushes basking in the hot sun, I heard the clink of the pole on the rocks, and soon the Lady Emma appeared slowly picking her way through the rapids. Presently she shot beneath the bridge and Jot landed out on a large rock on the right bank just above the Grand Pitch.

He did not say much about the place except that there was "some great kywashing around up there," and that the worst of it was not in sight. Several times, he said, when he put his pole down the whole length it did not touch bottom — a great danger when all may depend on getting pole-hold and snubbing at that particular place. Pointing to the last rapid above the Grand Pitch, the worst of those in sight, he said that he went through several places as bad as that. Many expert watermen would not have cared to run Grand Falls this year when Jot did. Let me forestall the question by confessing that I am altogether too much of a coward to have desired any part in it myself.

We took time to view the Grand Pitch from the dam both above and below and also crossed the stream to the left side where there is a great, square, out-hanging rock, which some poor witling undoubtedly either has named or will name the Devil's Pulpit. Let it be named Joe Mitchell's Rock, for here it was, in full view of the magnificent panorama of the river, the falls and the mountains below, that old Joe used to have his camp and his eel-pots, and here was enacted that laughable story with which many an audience has since been entertained, of Joe Mitchell's eels and Stickney's cow.

Just before we embarked, I found a family of snakes coiled up in the sun. It was mean to do it, but I threw them into the swift current to see them swim. They came straight to the shore, riding on the surface of the swift water, their heads and breasts reared up, their backs arched in undulating advancing curves. They were Virgil's pythons coming from Tenedos, vindicating his description point for point, and imparting to it a new forcefulness, it seemed to me.

From the Grand Falls down the stream is quiet, with low banks and few camping places. The hot sun made it pleasant for us, but in the treetops we could hear a wind howling. We glided along quietly, occasionally scaring up an old heron that would keep just within tempting gun shot of us, until we came to Spawnook Lake,[87] which is threaded on the stream like a single great bead. On the lake it was blowing a gale. From the shelter of the inlet we could see the big, white-capped waves, black and ridgy, rolling in to us across the shoal ground.

On a lake one never sees the smooth, glassy, green rollers of the sea shore; lake waves are blue, black, or leaden, with wrinkled fronts, and they rise up very straight on the foreside as they are driven on by the wind which they never long outlive. We looked at the lake before we started out, and planned how we should be able bear up against the wind. But this was not like that day when we were windbound at Nicatowis, nor like that other when we were driven down upon the shoal and rocky

[87] First mentioned in Chapter I, now, Saponac Pond on Gazetteer map 34. Here, Mrs. Eckstorm elaborates on the name.

ground at the foot of Caucomgomoc with the odds against us. We could see the worst of the waves, and the lee shore was clear sand. We laughed as, within the haven of the inlet, we took off our head gear to prevent its being blown away, tucked the tent down over the load and the gossamer over myself to keep the water off, and put out.

It was rough, about as rough as it could be on a lake no larger than Spawnook, and hard work for the paddlers, who had to do their best to prevent being driven back on the shoal ground and capsized. For I, it was good fun as the passenger with nothing to do but be rocked like a seagull and admire the skill with which the Lady Emma was held on her quartering course so long as the wind permitted. And the moment a gust came, or a larger wave than common lifted his crest, she was turned head to, and eased off, so that with an uplift of the bow she rode out what would otherwise have come near to upsetting her.

Maps give this lake the name of Saponic, but that is not its proper title. The real name is Pawnook, or Barnook, and it means "an opening in the mountains" — an appropriate name for this sudden expansion of the stream just as it reaches the foot of the massive Passadumkeag Mountain sloping down to it on one side, and the granite studded hills which encircle it on the others.

Pawnook was the name the Indians gave it seventy years ago. In 1828, or within a year of that date, my grandfather went up the Passadumkeag with some Indians and S. R. Peale of Philadelphia (a member of Long's expedition in 1819-1820, and of Commodore Wilkes's in the forties) and the Indians gave this name and this meaning. If we cannot restore the old Pawnook or its softer equivalent, Barnook, let us keep the vulgar Spawnook, and not give up name, association, meaning and everything for the barbarous Saponic proposed by some unknown mapmaker, or corrupted by some careless printer.

The wind was so strong that we could not keep the course we wished to. Instead of going directly for the old bark landing on the left where we intended to camp, we were forced to head up into the wind a great deal more than we wished to, until, when nearly half a mile out from the shore, where we wished to land, we could take advantage of a lull, turn and run in shore. We did not take in much water after all, thanks to good management. And we did pass a very pleasant evening on that campground; though being the last, it seemed just a little lonesome.

> *We were wrecked in the waste of waters,*
> *We were whirled in the storms like foam,*
> *We were beaten and tossed from the shores of rest,*
> *But tonight we are nearing home.*
>
>   from "*At Last*"
>   by Anna Boynton Averill

Fannie Hardy, 1891.

Photo taken by Manly Hardy at the last dinner on the
Passadumkeag. Fannie is holding the pheasants that would be
their meal.

Photo Courtesy of Digitalcommons, the University of Maine Library.

XXIV — "AND SO HOME."

"How many associations cluster around that little word.
Home Sweet Home.
O, I hope I shall find it as I left it."
Manly Hardly
The ending note in his 1858 Journal.

THE next morning we started out again — another glorious day, bright
October weather, not too cold, but every morning the trees waking to
find themselves redder than before. Just as we entered the outlet Father
killed two wood-ducks at a shot. A little below comes the fall called
White Horse, which Father and I walked past as only one man was
needed in handling the canoe and our extra weight would make it harder.
I remember that I had been allotting on the fun of running the quick water
here and at Lowell and lost both.

Many were the pleasant reminiscences of this day, little things seen
in passing — a blackbird in the bushes, a flock of ducks flying, ship-
timber floating slowly downstream, an old heron that like all those we
had seen this trip was so tame that we repeatedly came within a few rods
of him. At one place we heard drumming. While Jot and I remained in
the canoe looking over the side at the wriggling creatures in the water,
Father went off after the partridge. In the course of half an hour he
returned with his bird, having successfully located him and hunted him
up when he was drumming on the top of a granite rock some five feet
high.

Down to Lowell we floated quietly, but below there the stream is
broken by many rips, "nothing at all for water," as Jot would say, but
very delightful for the canoeist, who loves to feel the quickened pulse of

the water and to see the canoe, skillfully guided, swerve, turn, or shoot ahead as directed. Most of these rips had water enough on them to be run on the paddle, but sometimes we used the pole a little. With a poor canoeman in the stern every one, insignificant as they were, would have been a fresh vexation, for we should have been run upon gravel beds, scratched over little stones and bumped on big ones, which hurts one's feelings more than it does the canoe. But with Jot all was different. He does not need our commendations as woodsman, hunter, waterman, cook, or honest man, but he has them, none the less.

O, the perfection of a day, the perfection of a cruise — to glide over still waters in the hot sunshine, to dance with the ripples down the rapids, the trees standing on both sides robed in scarlet. That it was the last day, so soon to be over, only made us grasp the more greedily at its pleasures; we drank in our environment with the unslakable thirst of Gargantua,[88] and a hundred pictures of scenes we passed are held in memory as vivid as the moment we passed them.

How we did enjoy the day! like others that had preceded, rainy and sunny alike. Looking back, we would not have had any of them other than as it was. The weather and the events seemed to have sympathized from the first; we saw each place in the mood most becoming to it. We would not for a world have missed the exquisite delight of that day about the Pistol region, and Fourth Lake would not have shown half its proper dismalness on any but just such auspicious days as we spent there.

Just above Rocky Rips, Father shot a sheldrake flying overhead and brought him down into the water. We saw him fall and swim a space; when we were almost upon him he disappeared. We searched everywhere for him, scanning the bottom upstream and down, to see that he was not clinging to the weeds beneath the water, and beating the banks

---

[88] One of the two giants depicted in the 16th century pentalogy of novels, "The Life of Gargantua and of Pantagruel," by François Rabelais.

to drive him out if he were hiding. Failing to find him, we went ashore to take our last meal together.

After dinner we went down stream over Rocky Rips, Lightning Rips, Scalp Rock — natives call it Sculp Rock. It commemorates some old Indian fight probably of the last century, and there was another at Spawnook — and over all the other numerous rapids on the way.

'Tis too bad not to tell a good joke on one's self. I was pondering over the escape of the sheldrake, going over all the possible escapes open to him, how he looked, how he was wounded, which way he went, and all that, when only a few feet from us a pickerel flipped out of the water with such suddenness that I was scared into speaking. Well, what did I say? What but, "There's your duck, Father," and got well laughed at as I deserved, for the duck had been shot miles behind and was either dead or recovering long before.

We went down through the wide meadows, the booms, the rafting-out place, to the town of Passadumkeag. It was not pleasant to see houses again. We always dread the coming back. But we repacked our goods into smallest compass, brought out the neglected clothes brush and clean but crumpled collars, straightened our hat brims and made ready to go down to the railroad station and so home, as loath to return as we had been anxious to go. *Sic semper.*[89]

---

[89] A more familiar quote in Latin is, "*Sic semper tyrannis,*" which translates literally as, "*thus always to tyrants.*" The fact that Eckstorm writes simply "Sic semper," could be loosely meant as, "Thus always." The direct Latin, would be, "*Ita semper.*" I feel the same with each trip to and from "The Maine Woods."

Here talk, nor toil, nor cares intrude.

On the calm tide we float and dream,

Down drifting gently with the stream,

Through the sweet haunts of solitude.

from, *Camp Solitude*
by Anna Boynton Averill

Down Drifting Gently With The Stream
(Editor's Collection)

APPENDIX I — LOBSTER LAKE

Lobster Lake isn't easy to get to. The shoreline is undeveloped, other than a few isolated cabins. Once there, the paddler is afforded a fine view of Katahdin and Sabotawan. The water of the lake is crystal clear thanks to the filtering by the aquatic bivalve mollusc (*Margaritiferidae*). The location is beautiful, peaceful and for many it holds many memories. The one thing this Maine lake never had, was the Indian name "*Sungegarmook.*" In the files of Mrs. Eckstorm is a letter from 1931, where she took to task the author of an essay about fishing, who gave Lobster Lake just such a name.

In the June 1931 issue of Harper's Magazine, Brendan Lee penned the article, "The Incompleat Angler." To confirm that Lee had not misconstrued our Maine Lobster Lake for some other, I located and purchased an original issue of the magazine. The issue arrived, from a distant State, packaged in a plastic sealed envelope. The pages were yellow, showing its ninety years, and it had the smell old magazines acquire, but overall it was in fine condition.

The article by Mr. Lee was included just as the cover image had advertised. The statements that Mrs. Eckstorm had quoted in her letter were there alongside clear evidence that he did indeed mean the Lobster Lake located in T. III, R. XIV WELS.

A draft of a letter from Mrs. Eckstorm, in which she took exception to the incorrect Indian name Lee applied, along with his wrong linguistic interpretation, is contained in the *Fannie Hardy Eckstorm Papers* collection at the University of Maine.[90] It is reproduced here as a means to further show the knowledge Mrs. Eckstorm held, and her expectations of correctness when it came to the Maine woods.

As the typed letter is marked with 'draft' and contains several handwritten corrections, the wording of the final version is unknown, or if it was even sent to Harper's Magazine, and if it was, if Harper's Magazine issued a subsequent erratum to the Lee article. (The editor of this book has not been successful in finding a correction published in Harper's Magazine.)

* Transcription of Fannie Hardy Eckstorm's Draft Letter *

In the June Harper's Magazine, in an article by "Brendan Lee," (a) name under which we recognize a former "nature-writer" of some years ago, the writer makes a statement (p.109) for which a due correction should be speedily recorded. He says:

"From it, [a pond], as of old, the brook flows northward through unbroken forest to Sungegarmook – a picturesque Indian name which by some linguistic lunacy has been translated into 'Lobster Lake.' In the Milicete tongue sunge means 'fish trap'; and the root mook for 'water' has such pleasant variations as garmook for 'broad water' and murmook for 'flowing water' and boomook for 'sounding water' or a waterfall".

---

[90] Eckstorm, Fannie Hardy, "Note on an Article in Harper's Monthly Magazine June 1931," (2018). Fannie Hardy Eckstorm Papers. University of Maine.

It would be a simple task to tear this information into tatters: —
for example, *mook* is not a root, but a locative ending; *boomook*
means nothing by itself, and never waterfall, it being a part of the
word Seboomook, or Sebemook, a large lake, long used for
Moosehead Lake, which was called Lake Sebem; and so with the
others.[91]

The point to insist upon is that there is no such Indian name for
Lobster Lake, or for any other Maine lake that we know, as
Sungegarmook; and that Lobster Lake is an original English
name and not a translation of any Indian name for the lake. So as
for (sic.) from being a "linguistic lunacy" there is a good reason
for the name, which should not be changed by theorists or
strangers.

Lobster Lake was so called from the tiny fresh-water lobsters
which are, or used to be, found there in numbers. I have never
seen them described in any book, but I have seen and handled the
tiny creatures, which escape general observation. Conditions
change so much that one cannot assert that the same living
creatures will continue to inhabit their old haunts after many
years; but I have turned to the journal of an old cruise in the Maine
woods, made many years ago, and am not speaking from memory
when I say that one day, while having dinner at the foot of the
Horse Race on Caucomgomoc Stream, my father said he would
see whether he could not find a fresh-water lobster to show me.
He looked about in the stream just below the little double pitch a
few feet high, where there was a wing-dam on the right bank and
a sharp ledge sending out a spur upon the left (all most likely

---

[91] See Moosehead Lake maps and names, along with Eckstorm's research
on the matter in, "*Hubbard's Guide to Moosehead Lake and Northern Maine
- Annotated Edition,*" Lucius L. Hubbard and Tommy Carbone, 2020.

changed now), and there he found the low heaps of sand and small gravel heaped up by the little shell-fish. Scratching about the mouth of an entrance, as one used to do to draw the big salt-water lobsters out from under rocks, he enticed the occupant to come out and caught him. "Although he was not more than two inches long" - - I quote the journal - - "he could nip sharply and took the aggressive. In all his motions he was precisely like the large lobster." I held him some time on my hand watching him. He had miniature "big claws" like the large lobster and frothed about the mouth, and was as active and ugly as if he had weighed two pounds. I returned him to the water again after examining him. I have never seen one on any other waters in the state, but I know that Lobster Lake got its name from these little fellows.

The Indian name for Lobster Lake is Pes'kébé'gat, of Hubbard's map of the Maine Woods. Thoreau understood Joseph Polis to pronounce it Beskabekuk – and he probably did so call it; but the words are the same to an Indian. In his, "Woods and Lakes of Maine," Mr. L. L. Hubbard gives two interpretations of this word and a description of the lake. *Bé'gat* is a word for "dead-water" in Abnaki and *Pes'ké,* (or pisca as we get it in Piscataqua and Piscataquis) indicates a "branching." Mr. Hubbard suggests that the word may mean "Split Lake, because a point partially divides it."[92] (Sic) Or the word may refer to the entrance of the outlet into the West Branch Penobscot. Conditions here are so unusual that this most likely gives the name, "Branch of a Deadwater." The outlet comes in almost at right angles to the course of the West

---

[92] Mrs. Eckstorm is not exactly quoting the Hubbard text in this section of her letter. For the exact replication, see, *"Woods and Lakes of Maine - A Trip from Moosehead Lake to New Brunswick in a Birch-Bark Canoe - 2020 Annotated Edition,"* Chapter II and Appendix I.

Branch and the fall is so slight that in times of freshet on the river, the river rises much faster than the stream and turns the current up into the lake, which will rise eight or ten feet about its usual level by the water pouring up into the lake instead of flowing down the river. Many years ago, a green hand on the drive was sent down to boom off Lobster Stream, in order to keep the logs from being carried up into the lake. He naturally supposed the stronger current marked the river and so he threw his boom across the main river and turned a large part of the drive up into Lobster lake, where they had plenty of trouble in getting it back again with the current against them.

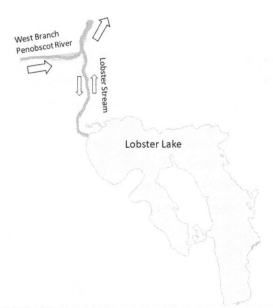

West Brach of the Penobscot and Lobster Stream
(Image added for illustration, not part of the Eckstorm letter).

I have known the name Mattahumkeag to be applied to Lobster Lake, which must refer to conditions at its outlet: it indicates that there is, or was once, a sandy point at the outlet. But the real peculiarity of the lake is that it is a "pocket-lake" or inlet-outlet lake, with a reversible current in the outlet, like Umbagog, Kezar Pond, Androscoggin Pond, Lovewell's Pond and perhaps other Maine lakes. I question whether the name Pes'kébé'gat did not apply exclusively to the stream, and perhaps Mattahumkeag to the lake above it, but it never was *Sungegarmook*.   F.H.E. (1931)

END OF LETTER

I should mention, that directly before Lee writes incorrectly this name *Sungegarmook*, by which some lunacy he has discovered, of which no one prior to he has heard, he states the following about the pond he is supposedly fishing:

"You may still find that pond, as lonely and alluring as ever, between the mighty shoulders of Big and Little Spencer Mountains. From it, as of old, the brook flows northward through unbroken forest to Sungegarmook – ."

Is it not interesting that Mr. Lee is concerned about the Indian name for Lobster Lake, but yet does not mention Kōkad'jo or Sabōta'wan – the rightful Indian names of The Spencers?

Following his mistaken identity for Lobster Lake, which we've covered, he continues:

"To my disappointment, the unnamed pond offered me no invitation to try my fly rod. Indeed, the water was hardly deep enough to cover the dorsal fin of a sizable trout, as I proved by drifting over it on a raft of cedar logs."

The 'unnamed' pond Lee mentions, depending if he was loitering north or south of The Spencers, given he writes, "between the mighty shoulders," could be either Kidney Pond to the north, or Lazy Tom Pond, to the south. On Hubbard's 1899 map, Kidney is not labeled and Lazy Tom Brook is shown, but not the pond; leading the reader to believe the 'unnamed pond' Lee refers to was what is now called, Kidney Pond.

The mention of Hubbard's book by Mrs. Eckstorm is important on several accounts. First, Lucius L. Hubbard was one of the foremost authorities on Maine Indian names throughout northern Maine in the 1800s and early 1900s. Second, the Hubbard map he compiled of the region was the definitive source for navigation, even according to Maine foresters, for decades.[93] And lastly, the letters between Hubbard and Eckstorm depict their friendship and mutual respect for one another's knowledge on the Maine woods. It is evident that she respected his work on the history of the Maine woods and Indian place names.

In Hubbard's book, "*Woods and Lakes of Maine,*"[94] Appendix I includes the derivation of the Indian name, and partially reads:

Pes'kébé'gat : Lobster Lake, near Moosehead ; "branch of a dead-water" ; from peské, "branch," and bégat, an inseparable for "water" (from nebpe, and literally "where there is water").

I, like Mrs. Eckstorm, wonder how this writer Brendan Lee, submitting an article to Harper's Magazine could have made such a linguistic mistake, given the numerous prior publications on the naming of Lobster Lake. As to the "fresh water" lobsters being in the lake, to that I have some firsthand knowledge.

---

[93] Kephart, George, S. "Campfires Rekindled. A Forester Recalls Life in the Maine Woods of the Twenties." Channing Books, MA., (1977). On page 49, "We also liked to check our map against published maps of the region, primarily Hubbard's Map of Northern Maine (1899), which was almost a bible map at the time." Also of interest is in his book, Kephart makes several references in his book to his time at Nicatous and Gassabais lakes.

[94] See the annotated edition from Burnt Jacket Publishing (2020).

During the summer of 2020, I traveled to Lobster Lake with my wife and daughter for a canoe excursion. From the south shores of Moosehead Lake, we did not take a steamer across the lake to the Northeast Carry and catch a transport from Mr. Morris to the Penobscot, as would have been done in the late 1800s.

We, unfortunately, took the longer way around. While we were in an air conditioned, high clearance, four-wheeled drive vehicle, the trip across the Greenville Road, north of Kokadjo and over Sias Hill to meet up with the Golden Road, was slow going and one I would not attempt again until I was reassured the rocks, boulders, trees, and two-foot-deep ruts have been removed from the 'road.' In all, the drive was over three hours long. I would have rather paid a handsome sum for a steamer ride and would have gladly carried the canoe the two miles to the river over the Northeast Carry, than drive that road again.

While at the lake we saw numerous fresh-water 'lobsters,' or as we call them, crayfish. So, in answer to Mrs. Eckstorm's uncertainty about the Lobster Lake lobsters still existing, they most certainly do. We also find them in abundance in Moosehead Lake. When young, my daughters would use a chicken bone as bait in a crayfish trap they'd set out by the rocks overnight. In the morning, they'd examine the tiny creatures, and when a pair were found, set them in a race across the rocks as they scrambled back to their home.

In addition to the freshwater crayfish, there are other interesting creatures at the bottom of Lobster Lake. While canoeing, in the clear water below, we spotted rows and rows of freshwater mussels in the sandy muck of the shallows. The clarity of the water in Lobster Lake, and many of Maine's lakes, depends on these mussels, which filter the water.

At the canoe takeout we came upon a group of five. They were proud to have 'procured' a bag of freshwater mussels for their dinner. While, these mussels may be edible with proper cooking, it should be told that the population of freshwater mussels on Maine lakes are dwindling, and when they go, so does the clear water. We thus would ask that you please leave them where you find them. Let's keep the water of Lobster Lake clear and be clear that the original Indian name for this body of water is - *Pes'kébé'gat.*

APPENDIX II — ECKSTORM ON THOREAU

Henry David Thoreau is mentioned five times by Eckstorm within this book. As would be expected, the Hardy family read Thoreau, his own books, the books published after his death, as well as his articles; in Chapter XX, Eckstorm mentions his essay, "Wild Apples."[95]

Fannie Hardy Eckstorm had a high regard for Thoreau. This is directly apparent in her statement, in Chapter IV, about Indian names, "The notable exceptions have been Thoreau and Mr. Hubbard, who have probably done more than all others taken together." However, Eckstorm also took a realistic view of what Thoreau had accomplished during his three trips to the north Maine woods.

In 1908, *The Atlantic Monthly* published the article, "Thoreau's Maine Woods," by Fannie Hardy Eckstorm in which she analyzes Thoreau's contributions, and attributions bestowed on him by others. It should be noted that Eckstorm frequently wrote book reviews, and by way of "letters to the editor," she issued critiques of stories that appeared in magazines. The essay included Eckstorm's retrospective on Thoreau's journals that were published after his death in the book, *The Maine Woods.* More so, her critique was of Emerson's eulogy of Thoreau.

In taking exception to particular words in the Emerson eulogy, along with Thoreau's own experiences in the Maine woods, Eckstorm evaluates Thoreau's writing for what is positive, as well as mischaracterizations she felt should be corrected from a historical perspective. While Mrs. Eckstorm was known to be critical of anyone who wrote about the Maine woods if she had reasons (and sometimes inklings) to believe they were incorrect, her essay on Thoreau is a critique of one of the most popular writers about the Maine outdoors. In

---

[95] Thoreau, Henry David "Wild Apples," The Atlantic Monthly, (1862).

Eckstorm's words, *"some one who knew their traditions should bear witness to Thoreau's interpretation of the Maine woods."* (Here, the 'their' she was referring to, were the Maine woodsmen.)

It is the purpose of this Appendix to examine the essay, Eckstorm's later correspondence on Thoreau, and the reception the essay received from a respected acquaintance of Thoreau, Thomas Wentworth Higginson. Letters have been discovered and journal articles published over the past century on the topic of Eckstorm's essay, to which time gives the benefit of further discovery and analysis.

The readers of this book, will know that Fannie Hardy Eckstorm knew the ways of the Maine woods of the late 1800s. Her depth of knowledge was acquired through her own experiences, her research, and the time she spent in the woods alongside her father before and after the Machias Lakes expedition. For most of her life, she studied Maine history with a particular focus on the traditions of the woods that she knew were fading, if not already extinct. As noted in the biographical sketch at the beginning of this book, Eckstorm was an accomplished figure in Maine history, a prolific writer, and well-positioned to speak her mind on the workings of the woods of Maine.

Mrs. Eckstorm was not one to shy away from controversy. Like her father, she called the situation as she saw it. As many who are experts in their field, she took errors as opportunities to make corrections. It was not her nature to let such misinterpretations stand. In the case of non-fiction, she took the words on a page literally. She not only took exception to published measurements of distance, or heights of mountains in the Maine woods (even though maps and survey instruments were what they were), she also disputed reported estimates of the size of canoes being built.[96] While Eckstorm was outspoken and often opinionated, her essay on Thoreau was written based on verifiable writings.

First and foremost, Eckstorm praises Thoreau's writing on the Maine woods. While quoting Louis Stevenson, who she notes has discarded Thoreau's book as "not literature," she states, "It is, however, a very good substitute," and, "it *is* the Maine woods. Since Thoreau's day, whoever has looked at these woods to advantage has to some extent seen them through Thoreau's eyes. Certain it is that no other man has ever put the coniferous forest between the leaves of a book."

In her most critical paragraph, Mrs. Eckstorm takes issue with the claims that Thoreau was beyond other mortals when it came to the craft of being a 'woodsman,' and in particular, a Maine woodsman. She writes, "There is a popular notion that Thoreau was a great woodsman, able to go anywhere by dark or daylight, without path or guide; that he

---

[96] In a 1945 letter to Donald H. Williams (*Colby College Quarterly*, Vol. 7, Iss. 1, 1965), she wrote of Thomas S. Steele, "The man is a liar." This was in response to Steele conveying his observation in his book, "*Canoe and Camera*," (1880) that at Hunt Farm a birch canoe of 28 ft. long and 4 ft. wide at midship was being constructed for artist Frederic Church. Eckstorm noted in her letter, "There isn't water enough in the East Branch to float such a leviathan – nor birch bark enough to make one of; and it would take a derrick to lift the thing." The accusation against Steele and the claim about birch, seem unfounded or without evidence. As an example, the birch bark canoe, "The Quebec" was built in 1860 and was 25 feet long. That canoe was run in a regatta on the St. Lawrence in honor of the Prince of Wales. It is said that the prince himself rode in a 40-foot birch bark. The camp of Frederic Church, which he named Rhodora and from which some buildings still stand today, is on the shores of Millinocket Lake. The canoe was not constructed for a river trip, but for use at Church's camp on the lake. In recent years it has become an artist retreat. (See, "Thomas S. Steele's Maine Adventures," by Tommy Carbone, 2021.)

knew all the secrets of the pioneer and the hunter; that he was unequaled as an observer, and almost inerrant in judgement, being able to determine at a glance weight, measure, distance, area, or cubic contents. The odd thing about these popular opinions is that they are not true. Thoreau was not a woodsman; he was not infallible; he was not a scientific observer; he was not a scientist at all. He could do many things better than most men; but the sum of many excellencies is not perfection."

This paragraph is so opinionated in wording, so damning against someone so popular in his writings of the outdoors and nature, it was certain to cause some Thoreau enthusiasts to be offended. Yet, had Thoreau ever claimed to be "perfect" as a woodsman? To understand her argument, we must go beyond the words of that paragraph to the details that Eckstorm lays down to support her points.

To begin, Eckstorm does not blame Thoreau for his elevated status in the knowledge of 'woodcraft.' Since Thoreau died at an early age, the majority of his woods-life was spent within a two mile walk of the village of Concord, Massachusetts, with short trips of exploration throughout his years. Given the facts that Thoreau borrowed an axe to build his cabin (a friend Eckstorm quotes in her essay noted, "a true woodsman *owns* his axe"), and he hired a guide to navigate the Maine woods, she questions how he could be elevated by Emerson to the status of a woodsman.

Of course, a "Maine woodsman" is characterized in the strict sense of her definition; men like the Penobscot lumbermen, or men like her father. When Manly Hardy and his partners went into the woods, for months at a time to trap and hunt, they went with the barest and incomplete maps (often none at all, as detailed maps had yet to exist for the deep-woods locations where they ventured in the mid-1800s), they carried few provisions, and they built their shelters by their own hands and their own axes. Thus, Eckstorm's comparison of a woodsman is to her defined standard, not to Emerson's, who she accurately stated, "lacked woods experience."

As for Thoreau himself, she writes, "(he) admits frankly, and sometimes naively, that he was incapable of caring for himself in the woods, which surely is the least that can be asked of a man to qualify him as a 'woodsman.'"

Of Emerson, she states, "For the over-estimate of Thoreau's abilities, Emerson is chiefly responsible. His noble eulogy of Thoreau has been misconstrued in a way which shows the alarming aptitude of the human mind for making stupid blunders."

We might excuse Emerson, for he was penning a eulogy,[97] but, Mrs. Eckstorm, who notes the eulogy was 'noble' and permits the poetic fervor of most it, takes critical exception to certain points. One such point is on Emerson's praise of the ability of Thoreau to measure distances. Emerson stated of Thoreau, "He could pace sixteen rods more accurately than another man could measure them with rod and chain."

The important words here for Mrs. Eckstorm, what she termed, *the fallacy of the significant detail*, were 'more accurately.' While Thoreau had been a surveyor, did Emerson have details of such experimentation to prove that Thoreau could pace out 16 rods (equivalent to 264 feet, or 88 yards, or 80.47 meters), more accurately than another man could measure them with rod and chain?

Eckstorm is not simply skeptical, she merely states, "that is nonsense, for it puts at naught the whole science of surveying." She sums up this section of Emerson's praise with, "the effect is agreeably artistic."

Another point of critical evaluation for Eckstorm is Thoreau's ability to navigate in the dark. Emerson wrote, "He could find his path in the woods at night, he said, better by his feet than his eyes."

Here, Eckstorm takes Emerson (correctly) as having been referring to the path Thoreau had worn to his own home at Walden, and not the

---

[97] Emerson, Ralph Waldo, "Thoreau," The Atlantic Monthly, August 1862.

backwoods of Maine. She counters, "There is nothing remarkable in this. How does any one keep the path across his own lawn on a black dark night?"

Eckstorm takes further issue with Robert Louis Stevenson who revised Emerson's statement, with his words about Thoreau's woodcraft as, "He could guide himself about the woods on the darkest night by the touch of his feet."[98]

On her critique of Stevenson's specific words and re-arrangement of Emerson's sentence, Eckstorm replies: "Here we have a different matter altogether. By (Stevenson) taking out that "path," a very ordinary accomplishment is turned into one quite impossible."

On the basis of how Thoreau had been characterized by Emerson and others, Eckstorm concludes, "Thoreau's abilities have been overrated." For the next five pages of her essay in *The Atlantic Monthly*, Eckstorm both praises Thoreau for his accomplishments and clarifies her criticism of content contained in the book, *The Maine Woods*.

While picking away at Thoreau's systematic knowledge to classify facts, she states, "he had not a particle." But, in defense of Thoreau, she writes, he wasn't so much concerned with the systematic facts, for example on the habits of a partridge chick his concern was with the "rare clearness of its gaze," not an ornithological study of behavior. Over and over, Eckstorm gives Thoreau credit for his observation and his keen interpretation of what he saw in the Maine woods, while at the same time criticizing his lack of exactitude from a scientific perspective. Her main thesis is that Thoreau's accomplishments in documenting his Maine travels do not elevate him to the position Emerson bestowed on him.

------

[98] Stevenson, Robert Louis, "Henry David Thoreau: His Character And Opinions." Cornhill Magazine, 1880. Of course, this essay was not written to praise Thoreau, and Eckstorm's critique is quite mild in comparison.

Eckstorm further clarifies, "It was not as an observer that Thoreau surpassed other men, but as an interpreter." To her, skills as an "interpreter," as applied to Thoreau, was a higher ability to 'see,' than merely one who observes. She continues, "He had the art – the art to see the human values of natural objects, to perceive the ideal elements of unreasoning nature and the service of those ideals to the soul of man." In this way, Eckstorm is elevating Thoreau for his more poetic side of his woods interpretations. She continued, "The power to see is rare; but mere good observation is not supernormal."

The analysis by Eckstorm may appear harsh, but that was not the purpose. In a letter from Donald Williams[99] to the *Colby Library Quarterly* (March 1985), he notes, "Her critique of Thoreau's *The Maine Woods* is well-known but it was never intended to be negative."

Anyone who reads the full Eckstorm essay, and knows her writing and position, would not interpret the article as negative. Rather, it was explanatory to properly define the scope of Thoreau's experiences in the context of woodsman versus observer, in specifically the *Maine* woods. Eckstorm pointed out the strengths of Thoreau in his characterizing the Maine woods, while critiquing the emphasis from others on his ability. Williams included a previously unpublished excerpt of a letter he received from Mrs. Eckstorm in 1945. She wrote, "Thoreau was a prophet – like that earlier race of prophets of the Bible, Elijah and Elisha, who did not foretell, but who *saw* what was about them and the trend of

---

[99] Donald Williams became friends with Eckstorm in her final years. Williams had an interest in Maine history and he had contacted Eckstorm, who responded in kind. The two exchanged letters and Eckstorm sent him books from her personal library, and even went out of her way to acquire texts she recommended he read. Williams donated much of the personal correspondence to the Colby library, an institution Eckstorm praised in a letter to him.

coming events. If only people would read Thoreau and not twaddle about him!"

In her statements, we read her frustration over Emerson's 'twaddling' in his writing of what she considered 'nonsense' in elevating the accomplishments of Thoreau beyond what she considered factual and realistic representation.

She perceived that Emerson, "demand(ed) the honors of a professional," in the realm of Thoreau being considered a woodsman, ornithologist, and botanist. But she is realistic, admitting, "On the other hand, because he made some mistakes, in, unimportant details, he must not be accused of being unreliable." Rightfully, she calls out how he catalogued his visit and how, although he may not have spoken to every man he journaled about on his travels through Maine, Eckstorm through her research and experience in the woods, states: "How trustworthy Thoreau is may be known by this, – that fifty years after he left the state forever, I can trace out and call by name almost every man whom he even passed while in the woods. And that cannot be done with a slip-shod record of events. The wonder is not that Thoreau did so little here, but that in three brief visits, a stranger, temperamentally alien to these great wildernesses, he got to the heart of so many matters."

Is that not a true tribute to the man and his accomplishments in what he did? It is illustrative to look at the amount of time Thoreau spent actually deep in the Maine woods. We must remember, at the time he traveled to Maine, just getting to the "woods" was a long-involved journey on trains, stages, and steamers.[100] His eighteen total days in the deep woods occurred over his three trips during 1846, 1853, and 1857, catalogued as follows:

---

[100] Thoreau, Itineraries & Trail Map by Maine Woods Forever. https://mainewoodsforever.org/ Cited Feb. 2021.

1846: August 31-September 11: His first excursion to Ktaadn – 12 days overall inclusive with travel, of which six days were in the Maine woods from Sept. 4 – 9.

1853: September 13-27: His second trip where he went to Chesuncook Lake with Penobscot guide Joe Attean – 14 days overall inclusive with travel, of which four days were in the Maine woods from Sept. 16 – 20.

1857: July 20-August 8: His third and final trip to the Maine woods, where he went farthest north to Eagle Lake in the Allagash with Penobscot guide Joe Polis – 19 days overall inclusive with travel, of which seven days were in the Maine woods from July 25 – Aug. 1.

It appears that Eckstorm was not the only person to have critical thoughts about both Thoreau's *The Maine Woods*, and Emerson's eulogy. The well-respected Thomas Wentworth Higginson (1823 – 1911), a Unitarian minister, author, abolitionist, early supporter of women's rights, and decorated soldier wrote about Thoreau in his essays on American authors.[101] It has long been believed that Higginson knew Thoreau, and their relationship is mentioned in Higginson's writings. How often and to what depth the two conversed is a matter of debate.

Higginson married Mary Channing, the sister of Thoreau's friend, William Ellery Channing, the poet, frequent walking companion of Thoreau at Walden Pond, and along with Sophia Thoreau the editor of

---

[101] Higginson, T. W., "Short Studies of American Authors," Lee and Shepard, Publishers. Boston, 1880.

the 1964 edition of, *The Maine Woods*,[102] published based on Thoreau's journals after his death.

Higginson and Thoreau are certainly thought to have been acquaintances, with mounting evidence they had a deeper friendship. This could explain why Higginson, had never made public mention of his thoughts on the characterization of Thoreau's posthumously published works, and the Emerson eulogy as he later did in his 1908 personal letter to Eckstorm.

Higginson did, however, provide a study of what he felt were mischaracterization of Thoreau by James Russell Lowell[103] and Channing. In his essay Higginson wrote of Thoreau, "I have myself walked, talked, and corresponded with him and can testify that the impression given by both of these writers (*Lowell and Channing*) is far removed from that ordinarily made by Thoreau himself." It appears Higginson was one who cut through a lot of the misconceptions being published about Thoreau from both opponents and proponents to focus on what he felt were Thoreau's true characteristics. Higginson summarizes that Thoreau was not living a 'wilderness' life of utter simplicity. He writes, "(he was) a young man living in a country village; (who) takes it into his head to build himself a study ... in the woods, by the side of a lake; He is not really banished from the world, nor does he seek or profess banishment; indeed, his house is not two miles from his mother's door; and he goes to the village every day or two, to hear the news. In this quiet abode he spends two years, varied by an occasional excursion into the deeper wilderness at a distance." The mention of

---

[102] Thoreau, Henry David, "The Maine Woods," Ticknore & Fields, 1864. Editors: Sophia E. Thoreau and William Ellery Channing. Sophia Elizabeth Thoreau was the sister of Henry Thoreau.
[103] Lowell submitted his analysis of Thoreau to the North American Review in 1865, after Thoreau had died.

'occasional excursion into the deeper wilderness' is interesting in the context of the Eckstorm critique as noted by the durations mentioned earlier.

Higginson had analyzed Thoreau's experiment in an unbiased way. So when Eckstorm characterized Thoreau as, "a good pasture man," who "never got to feel at home in the Maine wilderness," Higginson was not offended, he did not go on the defense of Thoreau as he did with Lowell and Channing, rather, he wrote to her. Excerpts from the letter read as follows:

> August 10, 1908
> Dear Miss Eckstorm
>
> Allow one of the very oldest of contributors (still living) for *The Atlantic Monthly* to thank you heartily for the best paper in the August number – your review of his "Maine Woods." I knew Thoreau well and was one of the most devoted readers of his "Concord & Merrimac Rivers," but have never seen his limitations so skillfully analyzed. More over I take especial interest in your Katahdin stories, having been there myself once an humble explorer there, at an early period.
>
> Very cordially yours,
>
> Thomas Wentworth Higginson (age 84)
>
> *(The full letter is also available in "Katahdin, Pamola & Whiskey Jack – Stories & Legends from the Maine Woods," by Tommy Carbone.)*

It should be noted that Higginson made a trip to the Maine woods and climbed Katahdin. He wrote about this excursion, of which he was very proud to have five women along, in a story published in 1856.[104]

---

[104] Unsigned, "Going To Mount Katahdin," Putnam's Magazine (1856). Higginson confesses his authorship of this piece to Eckstorm in his letter of 1908.

The original of the signed 1908 Higginson letter was sent from Mrs. Eckstorm to Donald H. Williamson in 1945, a few years before her death. Williamson did not publish the letter until 1965 when it appeared in the *Colby Library Quarterly*. The letter was known at least twelve years prior because Elizabeth Ring mentioned the comments from Higginson in her 1953 essay. Ring had corresponded with Eckstorm directly, and while Ring mentions the Higginson commendation in her paper, she was not in possession of the letter. Eckstorm later sent the original to Donald Williams.

These connections are all very interesting, and the analysis of the published works following the death of Thoreau are enlightening. It seems he struck a chord in more ways than one with many people, and isn't that the job of a writer? a poet? a prophet?

Additional comments from Eckstorm's essay illustrate how much she appreciated the writing from Thoreau. She wrote of him:

"It is the philosophy behind Thoreau's words, his attempt to reveal the Me through the Not Me, reversing the ordinary method, which makes his observations of such interest and value."

"Hardly would the chance tourist see so much."

"Thoreau stood at the gateway of the woods and opened them to all future comers with the key of poetic insight."

"Thoreau's prose stands in a class by itself."

On prose, Eckstorm did agree with Emerson on Thoreau's poetic side, even if according to Emerson, "His own verses are often rude and defective." Her essay's ending statement, on the poetry of, *The Maine Woods*, is a glowing appreciation of what Thoreau accomplished. The words of her conclusion, in the hands of a jilted and biased reader may seem harsh and the meaning lost, but she emphasizes just how valuable Thoreau's writing contributions on the Maine woods were.

"Judged by ordinary standards, he was a poet who failed. He had no grace at metres; he had not aesthetic softness; his sense always overruled the sound of his stanzas. The fragments of verse which litter his workshop remind one of the chips of flint about an Indian encampment. They might have been the heads of arrows, flying high and singing in their flight, but that stone was obdurate, or the maker's hand was unequal to the shaping of it. But the waste is nothing; there is behind them Kineo that they came from, this prose of his, a whole mountain of the same stuff, every bit capable of being wrought to ideal uses."[105]

In a final note, showing no professional misgivings on the Emerson eulogy of Thoreau, she began her text, "The Bird Book," published in 1901, with this Emerson quote:

"His interest in the flower or the bird lay very deep in his mind, — was connected with nature, — and the meaning of nature was never attempted to be defined by him. He would never offer a memoir of his observations to the Natural History Society. *'Why should I? To detach the description from its connections in my mind would make it no longer true or valuable.'*"

— Emerson on Thoreau.

(quoted at the beginning of, "The Bird Book.")

This appendix on Eckstorm's critique of *The Maine Woods* and of Emerson's characterization of Thoreau, is included in this book for the

---

[105] Mount Kineo, at the center of Moosehead Lake, is said to be the largest known deposit of rhyolite in the world. The rocks that form the cliffs of Kineo are a volcanic rock rich in silica. It was commonly called 'flint.' The high silica content results in conchoidal fracturing, which makes the rock easier to shape. For this, Native Americans sought out the rock to fashion tools and weapons. Source: Maine Geological Survey, 2018.

following reasons. First, this is a book about the Maine woods by Fannie Hardy Eckstorm. She did not claim to be a Maine woodsman, she was guided by her father, and she is quick to point out how little she was permitted to do on their Machias Lakes expedition. However, she expects the reader to know her father was a Maine woodsman and she respected him and the many others who possessed wood-craft skills.

Second, the Thoreau essay by Eckstorm is an important piece of her writing. She wrote *The Atlantic Monthly* article in 1908, forty-four years after *The Maine Woods* was published, and two years prior to the death of her father, Manly Hardy. This is likely not a coincidence and assuredly the content was discussed between the two of them for many years.

Lastly, this is the first known collective analysis of the various articles and letters on this topic. It is fitting to include them to provide a fuller picture into the writings of Fannie Hardy Eckstorm.

APPENDIX III — SELECTED REFERENCES

1. Averill, Anna Boynton, "Birch Stream And Other Poems." Maine: The Cricket Club, 1908.

2. Burnham, J. B., "A Winter Hunt With Jock Darling." Forest and Stream, January 1896.

3. Carbone, Tommy, "Thomas S. Steele's Maine Adventures," Two Book Collection. Maine: Burnt Jacket Publishing, 2021. *Includes excerpts of John Way's book.*

4. Eckstorm, Fannie Hardy, "Thoreau's "Maine Woods." The Atlantic Monthly, August 1908, pp. 242-249. (*Misspelling of her first name for this article was listed as "Fanny," This is the only time in all her contributions to the Atlantic Monthly this error occurred. Eckstorm never professionally, or personally, in her archived correspondence went by such a corruption to her name. It is surprising to find no correction in the Atlantic Monthly for this error.*)

5. Eckstorm, Fannie Hardy, "A Letter to the Editor." The Atlantic Monthly, February 1912, pp. 287-288. (Used as way of example.)

6. Eckstorm, Fannie Hardy, "Manly Hardy." The Journal of the Maine Ornithological Society, Vol. XIII, No. I., March 1911, Pg. 1-9. A tribute to the life of Manly Hardy.

7. Eckstorm, Fannie Hardy, "Six Years Under Maine Game Laws." A series of articles. Forest and Stream, 1891.

8. Eckstorm, Fannie Hardy, "The Bird Book." Boston: D.C. Heath & Co., 1901.

9. Eckstorm, Fannie Hardy, "The Death of Thoreau's Guide." The Atlantic Monthly, June 1904, pp. 736-745.

10. Eckstorm, Fannie Hardy, "The Penobscot Man." Boston and New York: Houghton, Mifflin and Co., 1904.

11. Eckstorm, Fannie Hardy, "The Woodpeckers." Boston and New York: Houghton, Mifflin and Co., 1901.

12. Eckstorm, Manly. "The Otter," Forest and Stream, March 4, 1911, Vol 76, No. 9, pg. 330.

13. Forest and Stream, "Death of Jock Darling," Obituary Notice. January 1898.

14. Hubbard, Lucius L., and Tommy Carbone, "Hubbard's Guide to Moosehead Lake and Northern Maine - Annotated Edition." Burnt Jacket Publishing (2020).

15. Hubbard, Lucius L., Tommy and Carbone, "Woods and Lakes of Maine. A Trip From Moosehead Lake To New Brunswick In a Birch-Bark Canoe. Annotated Edition." Burnt Jacket Publishing (2020).

16. Ring, Elizabeth, "Fannie Hardy Eckstorm: Maine Woods Historian," The New England Quarterly, 1953.

17. The Aledo (Illinois) Democrat, "Machias Lakes Monster," Dec. 9, 1881.

18. The Machias Union, "Chain Lake Snake," March 1882.

19. Vickery, James B., "Jock Darling: The Notorious "Outlaw" of the Maine Woods." Maine History, Vol. 41, No, 3 (2002). Compiled by Richard W. Judd.

20. Williams, Donald H., "Lady Of The Woods: Some Correspondence Of Fannie Hardy Eckstorm." Colby Library Quarterly, March 1985.

21. Williams, Donald H., "T. W. Higginson on Thoreau and Maine, letter to Eckstorm." Colby Library Quarterly, March 1965.

About Tommy Carbone

Tommy Carbone lives in Maine with his wife and two daughters. He studied electrical engineering and earned a Ph.D. in engineering management.

He writes from a one room cabin, on the shores of a lake, that is frozen for almost six months out of the year, and moose outnumber people three to one. (I bet you can guess where that is...)

His first novel, *"The Lobster Lake Bandits – Mystery at Moosehead,"* has made those 'from away' want to visit Maine. It's a big state – come explore.

BOOKS FROM MAINE'S NORTH WOODS

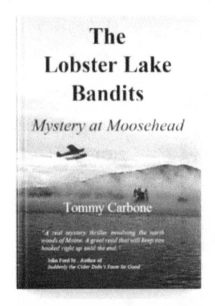

A Maine Novel

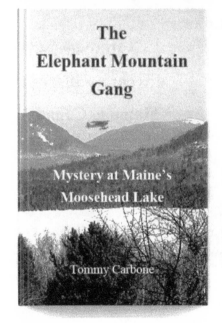

The second novel in the

Moosehead Mystery

series

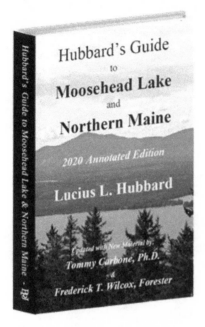

Hubbard's

Guide

to exploring

Northern Maine.

2020 Edition

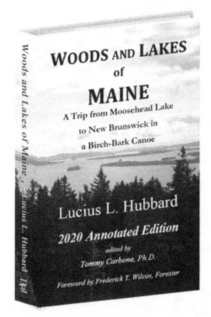

Hubbard's

adventure through

Maine to Canada.

2020 Edition

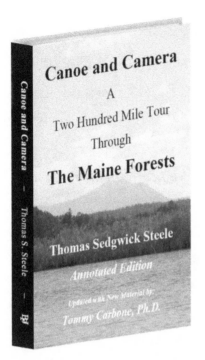

Annotated Edition

of

Steele's first

memoir from

Moosehead Lake to

Medway.

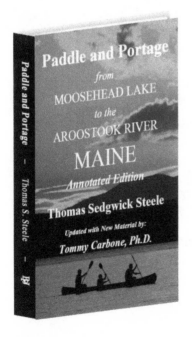

Annotated Edition

of

Steele's second

canoe trip memoir

from

Moosehead Lake to

Caribou.

"Thomas S. Steele's Maine Adventures."
This edition not only includes Steele's two books about
the Maine North Woods, but also bonus excerpts from
John M. Way's 1874 book,
"A Guide to Moosehead Lake and Northern Maine."

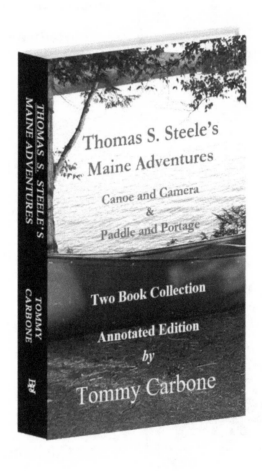

An annotated edition of additional stories from:

Fannie Hardy Eckstorm

&

Manly Hardy

Including full poems by Anna Boynton Averill

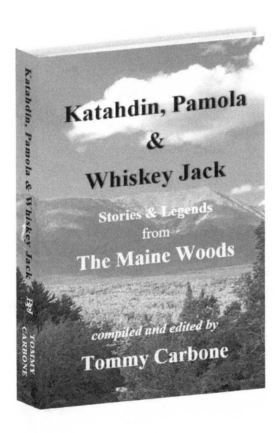

CPSIA information can be obtained
at www.ICGtesting.com
Printed in the USA
BVHW040951270622
640729BV00014B/183/J